SPIN

The Story of Michael Jackson

SPIN

The Story of Michael Jackson

Sherry O'Keefe

MORGAN
REYNOLDS
PUBLISHING

Greensboro, North Carolina

SPIN: The Story of Michael Jackson

Copyright © 2011 by Morgan Reynolds Publishing

Library of Congress Cataloging-in-Publication Data

O'Keefe, Sherry.
  Spin : the story of Michael Jackson / by Sherry O'Keefe.
     p. cm. -- (Modern music masters)
  Includes bibliographical references and index.
  ISBN 978-1-59935-134-6
  1. Jackson, Michael, 1958-2009--Juvenile literature. 2. Rock
musicians--United States--Biography--Juvenile literature. I. Title.
  ML3930.J25044 2011
  782.42166092--dc22
  [B]
                                        2009054191

Printed in the United States of America
First Edition

For Will and Beth,
Always with an open mind, on an open road

Contents

Statue of Michael Jackson in Eindhoven, the Netherlands, promoting the *HIStory* tour in Europe

Chapter One
One Red Guitar

> *When I found out that my kids were interested in becoming entertainers, I really went to work with them.*
>
> Joe Jackson

On June 25, 2009, the day Michael Jackson died suddenly from heart failure, the popular social network site Twitter crashed. The Web site of cable news channel CNN received more than 20 million page views in one hour, and for more than thirty-five minutes the world's largest search engine Google was unable to process the search requests for Michael Jackson.

The reaction to Jackson's death was overwhelming despite the fact he had not released an album since 2001 and that album, *Invincible*, had been a failure in the marketplace. It had been nearly twenty years since he had ruled the world of pop music and earned the title the "King of Pop," and his last years were filled with scandal and notoriety instead of musical success. But Michael Jackson still commanded the attention, and love, of pop music fans throughout the world.

When he died, Jackson was in the middle of preparing for his first world tour in years. A look at tapes made during his rehearsals make it clear why Jackson, despite all the controversy that had swamped him over the previous years, was still the "King of Pop." Released in November 2009 as the documentary *Michael Jackson's This Is It*, the movie demonstrates Jackson's genius as a performer. Clearly in total control of all aspects of the upcoming show, the fifty-year-old Jackson is seen correcting the moves of his back-up dancers, many of whom were nearly thirty years younger. On stage with a talented group of younger performers, he stands out as the one truly natural and gifted performer.

This Is It makes clear Jackson was ready for a comeback that would again electrify his fans. But it was not to be. The "King of Pop" was dead, tragically, and ironically, just as he was ready to return to the stage, the one place that allowed him to be who he truly was.

Music and performing had been a part of Michael Jackson's family for generations. In the late 1800s his great-great grandfather, Kendall Brown Scruse, was a legend in Russell County, Alabama. On Sunday mornings he sang hymns with the church choir, and people throughout the county and other parts of Alabama told stories about his strong and clear voice. When the weather was good, the church would open up the windows and Kendall's voice would ring out over the valley, rising above the other singers.

Kendall's great-granddaughter, Katherine Scruse Jackson, loved to tell her nine children stories of their legendary ancestor as she rocked her young children in her arms and sang them "Rock of Ages," "You Are My Sunshine," and "Cotton Fields" in a sweet soprano voice. She told them how Kendall had grown up as a slave for a family named Scruse, and how after the Civil War he'd worked on the Seminole Railroad with his own son and a grandson named Prince Scruse. Singing, she said, had made life and work more bearable to African Americans of Kendall's generation. Many of those old songs had been handed down through the generations.

Michael Jackson's earliest memories were of these stories and these songs. He loved the story and the songs and the idea that he was in the tradition of Kendall Scruse. His mother even told him that he had inherited his great-great-grandfather's voice.

Michael's father, Joseph Walter Jackson, was also musically talented. He was the eldest son in a family of five children. Joseph's father, Samuel, was a strict man who rarely allowed his children to socialize with anyone outside the home. When Joseph was a teenager, his parents divorced and he moved with his father from Arkansas to Oakland, California. After his father remarried for the third time, Joseph made the decision to move to Indiana and live with his mother and his younger siblings. There, he dropped out of school and became a Golden Gloves boxer.

While living in East Chicago, Indiana, Joseph fell in love with Katherine Scruse. Despite having a prominent limp as a result of childhood polio, Katherine was pretty and petite, with a warm smile for everyone she met. Katherine loved people and believed in strong family ties. Michael would later write that she "knew that her polio was not a curse but a test that God gave her to triumph over, and she instilled in me a love of Him that I will always have."

Joseph and Katherine were married on November 5, 1949, by a justice of the peace in Crown Point, Indiana. Remembering the pain of her own parents' divorce, Katherine vowed to herself then that she would stay married no matter any circumstances that might come their way. Michael's parents both agreed that they would surround their children with music. Katherine, a country western music fan, played both clarinet and piano, and Joseph considered himself a bluesman.

Joseph and Katherine Jackson, circa 1970
(Courtesy of Gems/Redferns/Getty)

In the 1950s, Joseph worked as a crane operator for a steel mill in Gary, Indiana. There were restrictions as to how many black workers were allowed to be employed at the mill. Black workers were also paid less than white workers. While he also earned extra income as a welder on the side, Joseph Jackson had a dream that he would rise above these restrictions by pursuing music in the evenings and weekends. The extra income was sorely needed and the creative outlet was important to him. He played guitar with his brother, Luther, in a band known as the Falcons.

The band played at local bars and for weddings in the Gary area. It had an electrical urban blues sound that was fitting for the 1950s. During the 1940s jazz had gone through changes. African American artists such as Charlie Parker and Dizzy Gillespsie had experimented with a more difficult form that came to be called "bebop," while many white musicians developed a lighter sound. Joseph's band played a funkier, hard bebop sound that combined rhythm and blues with bebop jazz. Joseph enjoyed his time with the band, but eventually the band failed, and he packed his guitar away in his bedroom closet with strict orders to his family that it not be touched.

Michael Joseph Jackson was born on August 29, 1958, the seventh of Katherine and Joseph's nine children. His oldest sister, Maureen (Rebbie), was born in 1950, followed by seven more brothers and sisters in rapid succession: Sigmund (Jackie) in 1951, Toriano (Tito) in 1953, Jermaine in 1954, LaToya in 1956, Marlon in 1957, Randy in 1961, and Janet in 1966. At one time, all eleven members of the family lived at 2300 Jackson Street in Gary, Indiana, one of the toughest cities in the U.S. As an adult Michael often described this house as being so small "you could take five steps from the front door and you'd be out the back."

With parents in one bedroom, the boys had the other bedroom with a triple bunk bed. Tito and Jermaine shared the top, Michael and Marlon shared the middle bunk. Jackie had the bottom bunk to himself. The three girls slept on a sofa sleeper and baby Randy slept on another couch in the living room. During the first years, the Jackson family often stayed warm by turning on the oven in the kitchen and opening its door.

Eight of the nine Jackson children. Top row from left to right: Jackie, Michael, Tito, Marlon; middle row from left to right: Randy, Rebbie, La Toya; front: Janet. Not pictured: Jermaine *(Courtesy of Pictorial Press Ltd/Alamy)*

After five years in this house, the Jacksons finally had a telephone installed.

When Joseph's band disbanded, he wasn't sure what to do. It was the early 1960s and Joseph, an enterprising man, noticed that singing groups were becoming popular. What he didn't realize at that time was that Katherine was taking his guitar out of the closet while he was at work. She would strum Joseph's guitar and sing country songs. She encouraged her children to join in. It did not take long before she realized her sons loved to sing and had good singing voices. Shortly after that, the boys began to sneak turns at playing their father's guitar. One day the inevitable happened. A guitar string broke. They all knew they were in trouble when their father got home.

Joseph was strict and his kids were afraid of him. He was quick to give his kids a beating if he felt they had done something wrong, and disobeying him was certainly reason enough for him to punish them. This time, it was Tito who was beaten because he was the one who had broken the guitar string.

After the beating, and after Joseph had calmed down, he asked Tito if it was true he had learned to play the guitar. Then he handed his son the guitar and asked him to play. As Tito played, Jermaine and Jackie gathered their courage and sang along. Although his daughters were also talented, what Joseph heard convinced him his sons could start their own singing group. The following night after work, he brought a red electric guitar home for the boys. Jackie was nine, Tito was seven, and Jermaine was six. The beginning of the group that would become famous as The Jackson 5 started with these three brothers.

By the time Michael was three, his older brothers were accustomed to rehearsing every day. These were happy times for the entire family. Michael would sit on the sidelines and study his brothers as they practiced. Although fascinated with music, he was even more intrigued by dance. Katherine would recall years later that when he was only eighteen months old Michael would hold his baby bottle and dance to the rhythm of the washing machine. She once woke him up at three in the morning so he could watch James Brown perform on a television show. This was one of Michael's earliest memories. James Brown was his inspiration. After establishing himself years later as a dancer, Michael said:

I knew every step, every grunt, every spin and turn. He [Brown] would give a performance that would exhaust you, just wear you out emotionally. His whole physical presence, the fire coming out of his pores, would be phenomenal. You'd feel every bead of sweat on his face and you'd know what he was going through. You couldn't teach a person what I've learned just standing and watching.

James Brown performs on the *Jerry Lewis Show*, 1969. *(Courtesy of Gary Null/NBCU Photo Bank/AP Images)*

Mid-1960s photograph of The Jackson 5. Front: Michael; middle row, from left to right: Tito, Marlon, Jermaine; back: Jackie *(Courtesy of Giles Petard/Dalle/Landov)*

Katherine realized Michael was different than her other children. He was shy and preferred to stay in the corner and sidelines and watch. He was, however, quick on his feet and often able to scramble out of the way of his father's fist. He was also the one boy in the family who dared to fight back against Joseph. Once, after a spanking, Michael took off his shoe and threw it at his father. He was only three years old at the time.

Joseph's anger and sternness created deep tensions in the family. In an attempt to bring some peace and reconciliation, Katherine joined the Jehovah's Witnesses. However, the conversion to a new religion didn't solve the family's problems. Jehovah's Witnesses do not celebrate Christmas, Easter, or birthdays and had other dictates that were almost as strict as Joseph's rules. Joining the religious group also helped to alienate the Jackson family from their neighbors.

The Jackson children were not allowed to play with other children before or after school. Their one opportunity to have friends and a typical social life was during normal school hours. All other hours belonged to music rehearsals and family chores.

One day, Katherine happened to notice four-year-old Michael imitating Jermaine as he practiced a James Brown song. His voice was strong and sweet, and he had such natural dance movements that he seemed much older than his age. Katherine realized that The Jackson 5 would soon have a new lead singer. When Michael started school that fall he demonstrated his singing abilities by performing the hit song "Climb Ev'ry Mountain" *a cappella* for his class.

Although neither parent wanted to hurt Jermaine by letting Michael take over the lead singer position in the group, Michael's natural talent could not be denied. In 1963, armed with a wide array of dance moves he had choreographed himself, Michael joined his brothers as a second lead singer for the group. He was five years old.

Joseph was relentless. When his sons weren't in school they were rehearsing. When they weren't rehearsing they were traveling to St. Louis, Kansas City, Philadelphia, and Boston to compete in talent shows. After winning several talent shows, they began to get jobs opening shows for groups such as The Temptations and Bobby Taylor and the Vancouvers. Michael would spend hours sitting to the side of the stage, hidden in the curtains, studying the vocal and dance stylings of the other performers.

One evening while waiting for the latest talent show to begin, Michael and his brothers overheard other contestants talking. They joked about needing to watch out for The Jackson 5 because the group was known to have a lead singer who was a midget. This caused Michael's brothers to begin teasing him. They laughed and called him "Big Nose" and "Liver Lips." It was true that Michael was so small that he was often seen standing on a milk crate to reach the microphone during harmonizing rehearsals with his brothers, but his feelings were hurt at being called a "midget." He was by far the most sensitive of Joseph's sons. He sought out his father and informed him that others were calling him a midget.

Joseph got down on his knees and hugged his young son and explained that it was a compliment that the other contestants were worried about the lead singer of The Jackson 5. He told Michael that it meant that he was a good singer. Michael protested and told his father, "They're talking bad about me." His father was gentle with him, but reminded him that this was how show business is. "This is only the beginning, Mike, so get used to it."

Chapter Two
My Poor Family

> *I'm going to make you the
> biggest thing in the world.*
> Berry Gordy

It was the dream of most aspiring black entertainers to have the opportunity to perform in the Apollo Theater in Harlem. Musical legends such as Billie Holiday, Louis Armstrong, and Duke Ellington and his Orchestra were only a few of the artists who had performed at the Apollo over the years. Accustomed to a high level of talent, the audience at the Apollo was notoriously hard to please. If they didn't like the entertainment on stage, they were even known to throw eggs and rotten tomatoes at the performers.

Michael was only nine when The Jackson 5 was first scheduled to perform at the Apollo, in 1967. He and his brothers felt the intense pressure as they took the stage to compete in an amateur competition. Their fears turned out to be unfounded. The audience loved the Jacksons from the moment the group began to sing. Joseph had entered the group in the highest

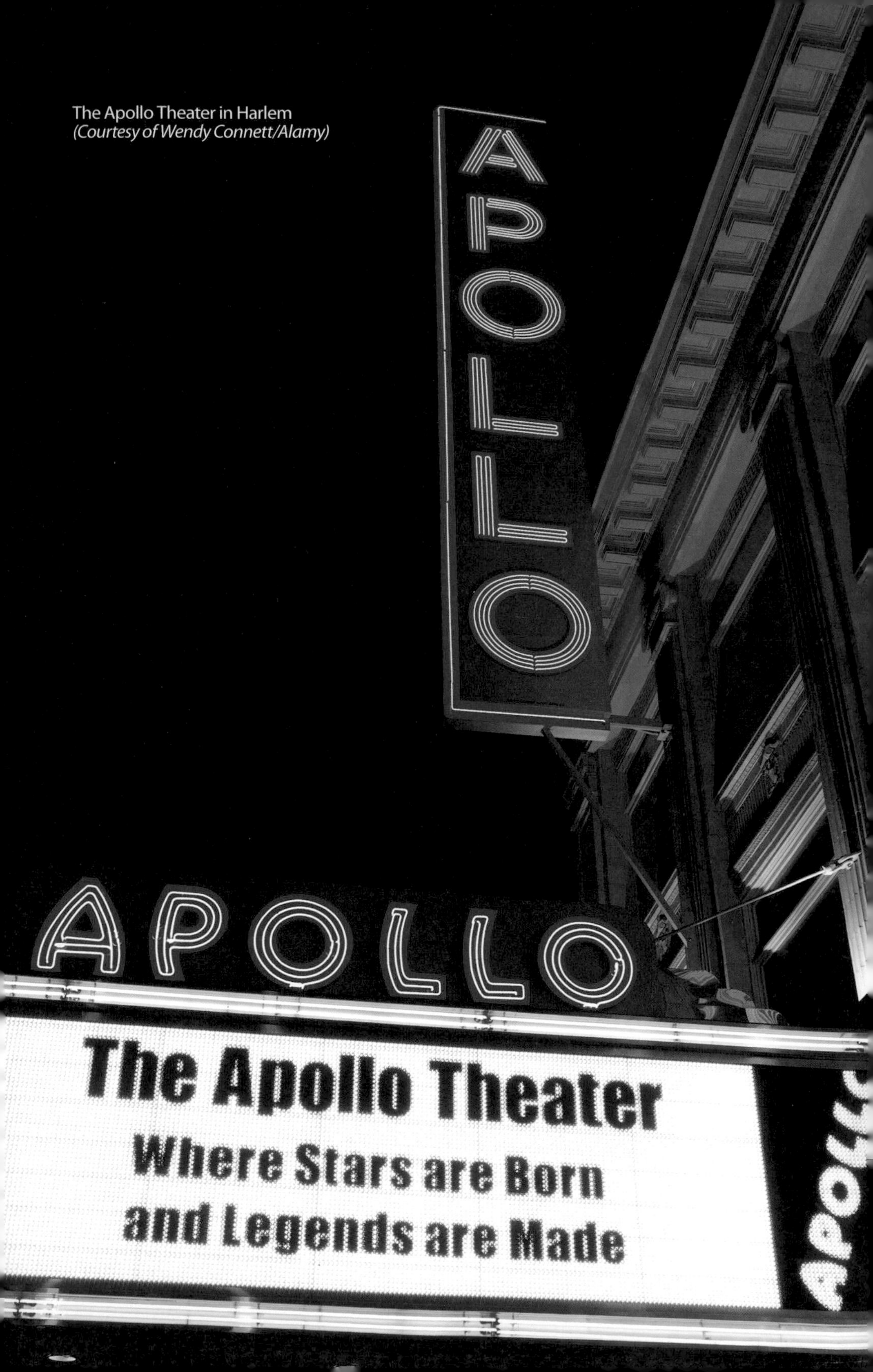

The Apollo Theater in Harlem
(Courtesy of Wendy Connett/Alamy)

level of the competition, the Superdog Contest, and they won. Winning at the Apollo lifted the group to a new level.

In 1968, Joseph made the decision to spend his time on the road with the band. This was a gamble with the family's future, but he felt that his boys were doing so well that they could now earn $600 per engagement.

The decision to risk everything on the singing group created even more stress in the family. Joseph responded by becoming even more demanding. The slightest mistake by any of them resulted in a spanking. Michael often fought back. "If you messed up during rehearsal, you got hit," he said later. "Sometimes with a belt, a switch. Once, he ripped the wire cord off the refrigerator and whooped me with it, that's how mad he was at me."

Of the five boys, Jackie was the eldest brother and the most passive. Tito was the one who looked most like Joseph. Although he could sing background vocals, studio musicians would eventually replace him on albums. Jermaine was the brother that Michael depended on in his early years. He wore Jermaine's hand-me-down clothes and insisted on having Jermaine next to him on stage. Marlon, whose twin brother died at birth, was highly competitive.

Life out on the road was not always the best place to be for five young boys. Joseph was willing to let them perform anywhere, at any time, which included strip joints and other unsavory "dives." Katherine was at home with the younger children, and Joseph was not concerned about what his sons were exposed to. Nine-year-old Michael would sit in the wings and watch how the men acted as women took off their clothes on stage. As the boys got older Michael often would be awakened when his brothers slipped girls into their hotel room.

Most hurtful of all, Joseph made no attempt to hide from his boys that he was taking other women into his own hotel room. Years later in a 2003 interview with British journalist Martin Bashir, Michael admitted that while he loved his father he also hated him for this. "My poor mother," he said. "My poor family. My poor, poor family."

Opportunities continued to open up for The Jackson 5. Joseph often had an array of decisions to make. Anxious to record, he signed a contract with a small record label called Steeltown. The Jackson 5 released two singles in 1968, "Big Boy" and "We Don't Have to Be Over 21." It was a thrill for the family to gather around the radio at home and hear their music on AM radio. Michael would remember it as one of the few times they still felt like one big happy family.

Soon afterward they were booked to perform at several prestigious locations. For the second time, they played at the Apollo. This time they followed Etta James, a legendary blues singer. Michael would always remember watching her perform—and she would remember him as well. During her performance, she was distracted by a little boy off stage watching her intently. Between songs, she went over to him and told him to scram. He left, but she soon saw him standing in front of the stage, still studying her every move.

After her performance, a visitor knocked at her dressing room door. It was Michael. He had come to apologize for disturbing her while she was on stage. Then he told her he wanted her to teach him what she did on stage. Etta James taught Michael a few tricks, and became convinced that someday this boy would become a huge talent.

In July of 1968, Bobby Taylor and the Vancouvers performed at Chicago's High Chaparral Club. Tommy Chong, who would later become a famous comedian, played guitar in the band. The Jackson 5 was the opening act and Bobby Taylor quickly recognized how talented they were. Although in years to come credit for discovering the The Jackson 5 and turning them into major stars would be given to several other artists, including Gladys Knight and Diana Ross, Taylor was instrumental in bringing the group to the attention of Berry Gordy, owner of Motown Records in Detroit.

During this period, both Stax Records and Chess had earned fine reputations for producing a more gritty and bluesy sound with African American artists such as Otis Redding and Isaac Hayes at Stax, and Muddy Waters and Chuck Berry at Chess. The founder of Motown Records, Berry Gordy, had a different idea on how to record African American artists. He wanted to make records that blended the "black sound" with a "white sound." His goal was to draw both a white and a black teenage audience. Gordy coined his approach "The Sound

Berry Gordy Jr. stands in front of Hitsville USA headquarters in Detroit, Michigan. *(Courtesy of Tony Spina/MCT/Landov)*

of Young America." He was also innovative in how he ran Motown Records. He modeled it after the auto assembly lines in his native Detroit. At Motown, artists would perform the songs written by a staff of writers. Gordy didn't want one single person to be involved in all the steps of making a record.

Gordy founded Motown Records in 1959. A former boxer, he brought the same pugnacious attitude into the record business. Soon he became the owner of the largest black-owned business in America at that time. Motown music was known for melodic hooks, simplified drum tracks, and easy to recognize lyrics. The company was soon producing such best-selling groups as Smokey Robinson and the Miracles, Diana Ross and the Supremes, and the Temptations.

Gordy believed in placing his stable of artists into competition with each other. Joseph Jackson had no problem with this strategy. He had always told his sons, "Either you're a winner in this life, or a loser, and none of my kids are losers." Studio time and songs from the staff of songwriters were dealt out at Motown according to which artists were having the most success. It was not until a group had gone without a hit for three months before a new group was allowed studio time. The Jackson 5 signed up with Motown and then waited patiently for their turn in the recording studio.

The late 1960s was a time of social and political turmoil in the United States. It was the era of the first moon landing and the hippie movement. The Vietnam War was intensifying and protests against the war were escalating across the nation. Old standards and prejudices were being questioned by the younger generation. The older generation, which had survived World War II and the Great Depression of the 1930s, was at odds with the newer generation.

Opposite Page: Album cover for The Jackson 5's first album, *Diana Ross Presents The Jackson 5*, released in 1969 (*Courtesy of Blank Archives/Getty*)

Racial equality was at the forefront of conflict. The changes wrought by the civil rights movement were painful and came at a high cost. Many white Americans were uncomfortable as minority groups stepped into roles previously restricted to whites only. Conventional choices were being questioned and overturned. In 1968, both the Reverend Martin Luther King Jr. and Robert Kennedy, who had long championed civil rights, were assassinated.

The Jackson 5 released their first album in this chaotic time, but, following the Motown model, were careful not to be seen as part of the social turmoil.

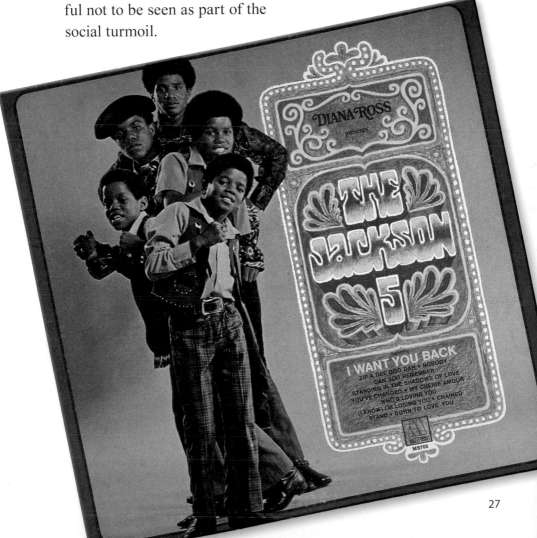

The Jackson 5 was an easy group for both whites and blacks to enjoy. They conveyed a friendly and peaceful idea of black pride, one that reflected kinship and aspiration rather than opposition. White America could easily embrace and appreciate the all-black singing group that competed with other popular white singing families of the era, such as the Osmonds, the Cowsills, and the Partridge Family.

Radio was the most popular way for groups to be heard in the 1960s and 1970s. There were only a few television networks in the country, but one of the most popular and prestigious shows was hosted by Ed Sullivan. Both Elvis Presley and The Beatles had burst onto the American scene when they appeared on *The Ed Sullivan Show*. In 1969, The Jackson 5 was asked to perform. The invitation was proof they were becoming widely popular. Ed Sullivan did not invite groups to perform unless they were considered sensational. Michael, with his sparkle and irresistible smile, was the star of the show. By the time they had performed their three songs, Michael had won the audience over with his clear voice and energetic dance moves.

The Jackson 5 released its first album in 1969. The single from the album, "I Want You Back," shot to number one on the charts. Before the end of 1970, three more Jackson 5 singles had topped the Billboard charts: "ABC," "The Love You Save," and "I'll Be There." Although this was an unprecedented feat, it was just the beginning of many musical accomplishments the group and Michael Jackson would enjoy in the years to come.

All was not perfect, however. Michael had yet to become a teenager, but was learning some harsh truths about the music industry and life. In 1968, after signing with Motown, the

Jackson family moved to Encino, California, where they lived in a large five-bedroom home. At that time, Diana Ross, who lived close by, was a superstar. She and the Jackson family quickly became close. Michael and Ross in particular formed

The Ed Sullivan Show featuring The Jackson 5. From left: show host Ed Sullivan, Jackie, Marlon, and Michael *(Courtesy of CBS/Landov)*

a lasting relationship, which would later result in Ross being designated as a backup guardian for Michael's children should he pass away. Ross took Michael and his brothers under her wing, watching over them and giving them advice on how to negotiate their way through the often cut-throat music industry.

A lesson about dishonesty in show business was learned when, prior to Diana Ross introducing the media in California to The Jackson 5, she showed the boys a telegram being sent out to the press inviting them to a party where the group would perform. The telegram read in part: "Please join me in welcoming a brilliant musical group, The Jackson 5, to Beverly Hills. The Jackson 5, featuring sensational eight-year-old Michael Jackson, will perform live at a party." Michael showed the telegram to Berry Gordy and informed him that a mistake had been made. He was ten years old, not eight. Gordy told him that from now on, Michael was to tell people he was eight years old and that Diana Ross had discovered The Jackson 5, which was also not true. It would make for better publicity, Gordy said.

Years later, Michael would share this story and recall, "I figured out at an early age that if someone said something about me that wasn't true, it was a lie. But if someone said something about my image that wasn't true, then it was okay. Because then it wasn't a lie, it was public relations."

Chapter Three
On His Own

> *I don't know if I can do this forever.*
> Michael Jackson

In the late 1960s and early 1970s the production of pop music began to change. Due primarily to the increase of competition, profits began to fall. Many record companies responded by eliminating their staffs of songwriters and production managers. Recording artists who could write their own songs were becoming more popular. However, this was a trend that Motown continued to resist. Berry Gordy remained convinced that the Motown model, where songs were assembled and the artists did not write their own songs, was the best way to make consistent hit music.

Berry Gordy did, however, make one major change. He moved the headquarters of Motown from Detroit to Los Angeles. Gordy was hoping to pursue filmmaking.

Gordy also kept the The Jackson 5 busy recording and performing. "I remember falling asleep at the mike," Michael would recall years later. Some songs were taped several dozen times and recording sessions sometimes lasted until two in the morning. While other kids his age were attending school during the day and riding bikes after school, Michael was either in recording studios or out on the road performing. The studio hired a full time nanny-tutor for the boys. Michael seemed happiest when studying other performers, or other segments of musical production. He claimed, years later, "Some musicians—Springsteen and U2, for example—may feel they got their education from the streets. I'm a performer at heart. I got mine from the stage."

Michael came to care for his tutor, Rose Fine, as did his brothers. "It was Rose who instilled in me a love of books and literature that sustains me today," he later wrote. He loved to read but did not care for schoolwork. Instead, he thrived on hard work, spending time in recording sessions seven days a week. Between working for Berry Gordy, whose idea was to breed a fierce competition between everyone at Motown, and having a hard-working, driven father, Michael inevitably was becoming a workaholic.

The Jackson family settled into life in Encino, a wealthy community about thirty minutes from Los Angeles. The move did nothing to change the control Joseph asserted over his children in Gary, Indiana. There was little time for any social contact with anyone outside the music industry. Each child was limited to five minutes on the family phone, and every month the phone company obliged the family by routinely changing the phone number.

Family closeness was more difficult to achieve in their new, larger house. The living room was twice the size as the old, two-bedroom house in Gary. Jermaine would later admit he missed the old house, recalling that in Gary: "You had to be close. You felt that closeness as a family. But in Encino, the place was so big we had to make plans in advance to see each other. I think that Michael, in particular, was unhappy there. He felt, as I did, that we were all losing touch with each other."

There was another source of tension in the family. One night The Jackson 5 was to appear on a national television show hosted by Diana Ross, *The Hollywood Palace*. As usual, Joseph was backstage, pacing back and forth, giving last-minute advice to each of his five sons. Meanwhile, Diana kept coming backstage to share private conversations with Michael. Finally, after speaking one last time with Michael, Diana returned to the stage. Then, waiting to go on from behind the curtains, the family heard Diana introduce them: "Let's welcome Michael Jackson and The Jackson 5!"

The boys rushed out on stage while Joseph fumed. He found Berry Gordy and complained about Michael being singled out from his brothers. Gordy told Joseph that Michael was the obvious star. Joseph insisted: "All the boys are equal. We're not singling Michael out from the rest. It'll just cause problems."

The Jackson brothers were portrayed as sons in a wholesome musical family. Ed Sullivan had been one of the first to promote this wholesome image when he had introduced them to the nation, calling them "fine young boys." They were appearing on the cover of major magazines and even had a cartoon show fashioned after them. Later, they would have a short-lived television program featuring the family.

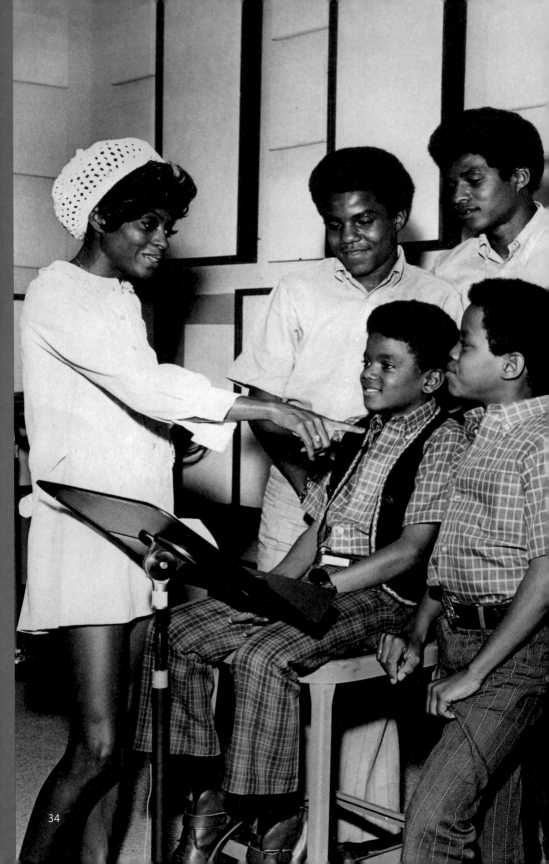

Michael might have been anointed as the leader of the group, but he was not as able to adjust to fame as easily as his brothers. In 1970, when he was twelve, The Jackson 5 made their first major concert appearance in Philadelphia. Whereas in the past the family would travel by van with their father, now they flew in chartered jets. When they arrived, more than 3,500 fans mobbed the Philadelphia International Airport, screaming and trying to break down fences. Security officers were belatedly called in to protect them from the overzealous fans. At the concert, more than one hundred security officers were required to continually push back the audience trying to swarm the stage. Back at the hotel after the show, Michael broke down. Jermaine remembered, "Michael was scared to death. The rest of us were more amazed than scared, but Mike was genuinely frightened. 'I don't know if I can do this forever', he said. 'Maybe for a little while, but not forever.'"

When The Jackson 5 performed at the Los Angeles Forum, they broke the venue's attendance record. During the show, after Michael told the audience that the next song they would be singing, "The Love You Save," had knocked The Beatles out of the number one slot, a large rumbling sound began

Opposite Page: The Jacksons with Diana Ross in 1970. Motown Records used Ross's fame to jump-start the Jacksons' musical career. Michael is seated beside Marlon in front, and behind them, from the left are Tito, Jackie, and Jermaine. *(Courtesy of Pictorial Press Ltd/Alamy)*

inside the Forum. The audience was rushing the stage. Row after row of people were being trampled. The Jackson 5 was forced to stop in the middle of the song and flee the stage. They were rescued by a security force just in time to avoid the dangerous crush of screaming fans.

Even in the midst of this chaos Michael's natural talent for song and dance became more obvious. It came to him naturally. He would later confess, "I'll tell you the honest-to-God truth. I never knew what I was doing in the early days. I just did it. I just felt the emotion behind it."

His ability to feel the emotion in a song was evident when his first solo single, "Got to Be There" reached the number four slot on the charts in 1971. Less than one year later, the album, similarly titled, climbed as high as number fourteen on the charts. This love song was one of the most desired songs in the Motown catalog, and many of the Motown artists were eager for the chance to record it. Initially, Motown planned for The Jackson 5 to record the song together, but both Joseph and Gordy were so pleased with Michael's voice it was turned into a solo project. At the time Joseph considered that this was just another way to make more money. Neither he nor Michael's brothers had any idea that this casual introduction of Michael

Courtesy of Michael Ochs Archives/Getty

as a solo artist would later result in him permanently leaving the family group.

In 1972, the year Michael turned fourteen, his solo song, "Ben," became a number one hit. Written for a movie with the

same name, the emotionally tense song was nominated for an Oscar. It was so beautiful it is easy to forget it is about a telepathic rat. Later, Michael's performance of this song at the Academy Awards in 1973 would be remembered as one of the most emotionally open-hearted performances he ever gave.

While Michael was happiest on stage, it was becoming obvious to his mother that he did not have what it took to deal with the pressure of success. She also knew she had no way to protect him. "If anyone in show-business history could ever be said to be lacking in 'people skills', it would be Michael Jackson . . . he doesn't really understand people, or even try to understand them, because when he was a youngster, he was surrounded, for the most part, by either showbiz kids or wealthy students who, like himself, were never exposed to the 'normal' masses."

The Jackson 5 performing on their European tour in 1972 *(Courtesy of Christian Rose/Dalle /Landov)*

Michael was the most popular of the brothers, but was also the one who lacked the skills to deal with popularity and fame. He began to show signs of deep insecurity. He always requested a body guard to sneak him in and out of the hotels by way of the freight elevators and kitchens. Many years later he would recall that he had stayed in the most deluxe hotels in the world, but he had never seen the plush lobbies, only the kitchen and back alleyways.

His mother's understanding was not enough to help him navigate the ever-increasing pressure of stardom. As his brothers continued to embrace the normal social aspects of life,

Michael became a loner. His mother knew how important his siblings were to him and she hoped that "as long as we all had each other, I figured we'd be okay. I prayed that we would be okay."

Katherine was wise to worry, as it would be impossible to protect her family and hold them together. In 1972, Tito announced that he intended to marry Delores Martes, a seventeen-year-old classmate. They had met shortly before the group became famous. Soon after this announcement, The Jackson 5 embarked on a twelve-day tour of Europe. Landing at London's Heathrow Airport, the group was mobbed by an uncontrollable crowd. Large chunks of Jermaine's hair were jerked from his scalp and Michael was nearly choked to death by over-eager fans. Later, fans barricaded the exits to Churchill

Founder of Motown Records, Berry Gordy Jr. *(Courtesy of Pictorial Press Ltd/Alamy)*

Hotel and trapped them inside. The police had to spray water at the mob before The Jackson 5 could leave the hotel.

The family received another shock in March 1973 when Katherine filed for divorce. She had learned that Joseph had fathered a baby with another woman. It soon became evident, however, that the family, and Michael, needed Katherine's steady presence more than ever. Realizing this, Katherine changed her mind about the divorce. She made the difficult decision to remain married to Joseph. Over the years, Katherine would be sorely tested in her marriage and would file for divorce several times, and then change her mind.

During this same time the family learned that Jermaine had fallen in love with Berry Gordy's daughter, Hazel. They were married in late 1973 in an elaborate ceremony with celebrities from across the world in attendance. A year later brother Jackie married his school-sweetheart, Enid Spann. Joseph had argued against the marriages but was unable to stop them. Jermaine and Jackie wanted a refuge from their father.

By 1975, Michael had lost respect for Joseph because of his numerous affairs and his violent attempts at controlling his maturing sons. Feeling that it was time to gain some distance from this turmoil, Michael hoped to pursue a more creative and individual path. He arranged to have his first private meeting with Berry Gordy. He was not yet seventeen.

Berry Gordy felt that Motown had made The Jackson 5 famous and said that if they left the company it would ruin both Michael's solo career and the group. Michael disagreed. He was sure he had the creative talent to write and produce his own music and that if Gordy would not allow him to do so that it was time to sign with a new label. "They [Motown] not only refused to grant our requests," Michael said, "they told us it was taboo even to mention that we wanted to do our own music."

Joseph was furious when he learned that Michael had talked to Gordy on his own, but he was in agreement with Michael about establishing creative control in their music. After a series of meetings with both Motown and other recording companies, Joseph agreed to have The Jackson 5 sign with Epic Records.

The signing bonus was $500,000 and Epic Records agreed to pay the group a 94.5-cent royalty for every album sold in the United States. This was a huge improvement from the 11 cents per album they had been earning at Motown. But, before the group could become too excited about this new contract, they were hit with bad news from Motown.

Having signed the Motown contract years earlier without reading it, Joseph did not realize that he had agreed that his group would have to pay all recording costs for each of their recordings. During the six years at Motown, they had recorded 469 songs, but only 174 of those songs had been released. This meant they still owed Motown over $500,000 in recording costs for songs that had never been released. While that was hard news to accept, the group was also told that Motown owned the name, "The Jackson 5." Once they left Motown they could not use that name for any commercial purpose.

Losing the name was a low blow, but the group decided that they would call themselves The Jacksons. All five boys gathered around their father to vote on the decision to switch names and to sign with Epic Records.

The opportunity to write and record their own music was an exciting direction for Michael and the group, but they paid a price. Jermaine had been torn between being loyal to his wife, Hazel, Gordy's daughter, and being loyal to his family. When it came time to sign the contracts, he refused and chose to stay signed on at Motown as a solo artist. Jermaine felt that the family had deserted him. The family felt that he had betrayed them by not leaving Motown. They added brother Randy to the group, but the pain of losing Jermaine to Berry Gordy, of having him choose Motown over his family, was deep. Clearly, the Jacksons were drifting apart professionally. But they had no idea how much wider and deeper the split would soon become.

Michael Jackson singing on stage in his hometown of Gary, Indiana. *(Courtesy of Trinity Mirror/Mirrorpix/Alamy)*

YOU ARE HERE

Michael Jackson as the
Scarecrow in *The Wiz*, 1978
(Courtesy of Photos 12 / Alamy)

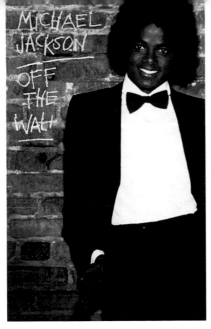

Chapter Four
Off the Wall in a Black Tuxedo

> " *I'm doing this on my own.* "
> Michael Jackson

In 1978 Diana Ross was cast to play Dorothy in *The Wiz*, a remake of the classic film *The Wizard of Oz*. The movie was based on a hit Broadway play of the same name and was produced by Motown and Universal Pictures. When it came to casting the other parts she was insistent that Michael be cast in the role of the Scarecrow. The producers agreed and Michael had his first film role.

Famed record producer and jazz musician Quincy Jones worked as the musical director on *The Wiz*, which featured an all-black cast. Among the musicians Jones had worked with during his career, as both musical arranger and producer, were such legends as Frank Sinatra, Ray Charles, Dizzy Gillespie, and Miles Davis. As he watched Michael Jackson rehearse his role as the Scarecrow, Jones recalled, "I saw a depth watching him . . . he knew everybody's dialogue, he knew everybody's song, he knew everybody's steps. I'd never seen somebody who could absorb so much so quickly."

During the rehearsal, Michael continued to mispronounce the name Socrates, which one of his lines included. He would say *So-CRAY-tees* instead of *SOK-ra-tease*. The crew giggled each time he mispronounced the name, but he did not know what he was doing wrong. When it became apparent that no one would help Michael out, Jones approached Michael and whispered "Sock-ra-tease, Sock-ra-tease."

Jones was impressed by the teenager's quiet demeanor. Later, when Michael asked Jones to help him find a producer for a solo album he was considering making, the two recognized instantly they would be able to work well together.

When Michael told his father that he planned to record a solo album, Joseph did not take the news well. Joseph had hoped Michael would come to realize that his place was with his family, both on stage and off. However, despite his doubts Joseph told Michael, "Do what you want as long as it doesn't interfere with group business."

The Jacksons had recorded an album, *Destiny*, and had promoted it on a

Quincy Jones
(Courtesy of George Brich/AP Photo)

tour in 1979. Compromises between his brothers, father, and the record company left Michael feeling dissatisfied and he had begun to think of doing an album on his own. Now he looked forward to trying his hand at another solo album and proving to both his family and the music industry that he was a star in his own right.

Initially, Epic Records was concerned about Quincy Jones teaming with Michael. They thought Jones was too jazz oriented. Michael insisted his new friend understood him and believed in his talent and potential. Jones, for example, realized that Michael was rhythmically driven and searched for songs to enhance this. He had a voice coach work with Michael, teaching him vocal exercises to help him expand the bottom and top range of his singing voice.

When the recording sessions began, Michael's preparedness impressed the studio musicians whom Jones employed for this album. Recording time in the studio was expensive, and Michael did his homework outside of the studio to save their time and money. When he showed up, his approach to the work was both dramatic and concise.

Michael was equally pleased to be working with Jones. Accustomed to years of strict discipline and a tense environment with his father, he thrived in the warm atmosphere Jones created in the studio. Jones was willing to try anything with Michael. He recalled that in the beginning, Michael was so shy "he'd sit down and sing behind the couch with his back to me, while I sat there with my hands over my eyes with the lights off."

The album they put together, *Off the Wall*, established Michael Jackson as one of the top musical artists in America. Jones would later come to think it was Michael's best work

Michael Jackson's 1979
Off the Wall album cover
*(Courtesy of GAB Archive/
Redferns/Getty)*

because Michael was relaxed and the album allowed for a free range of his talents. When performing with his brothers, Michael was explosive with the dance hits that had gained the group recognition, but both men had understood that the solo album needed something more. "The ballads were what made *Off the Wall* a Michael Jackson album," he said later. "I'd done ballads with [my] brothers, but they had never been too enthusiastic about them."

One song off the album, "Don't Stop 'Til You Get Enough," took less than three months to reach the top of the charts in 1979. The song features a playful falsetto voice that no one had ever heard Michael use before. This had been Michael's idea. The song was also the subject of Michael's first video.

The album cover featured Michael Jackson, handsome in a tuxedo and glittering white socks, announcing to the world that he most assuredly was not a midget with a great voice, but an adult breaking out on his own. The recording label claimed credit for dressing Michael in the tuxedo, but the white socks were an example of his own new fashion sense. The shiny white socks helped draw attention to his footwork when he danced in the video.

On August 29, 1979, Michael turned twenty-one, and he had a great deal to celebrate. His first solo album with Epic Records had sold more than 20 million copies worldwide and had produced four Top Ten singles, making him the first solo artist to achieve this in America. He was pleased to have successfully accomplished one of the goals he had set for himself. He felt this made him a real man because real men like Walt Disney and Fred Astaire, both of whom he admired, not only achieved their goals, but as Michael later noted "look at how much joy they gave other people. People looked up to them.

I want people to look up to me, too. They made paths. I want to make one, too."

Michael had learned what was required to produce solid music, and now he had come to understand that he would need his own lawyer in order to protect his interests. Joseph, as a manager for the group The Jacksons, made decisions Michael disagreed with. He needed power to fire his father and knew power meant money. If he had his own accountants and attorney to negotiate record sales, contracts, and publishing deals, he could insulate himself from his father.

He hired John Branca, a thirty-one-year-old lawyer with a background in corporate tax law. Branca was brought on board to help him achieve two goals: to be the biggest star in show business and to become the wealthiest. Branca responded with enthusiasm and loyalty. For the next twenty-plus years John Branca would be considered by most authorities as the most important person in Michael Jackson's career.

One of Branca's first tasks was to work out the details to ensure he would never be required to record another song with any of his brothers unless he wanted to do so. At any time, should Michael decide to permanently break from The Jacksons, the record company would be obligated to continue recording The Jacksons without Michael. It was important to Michael that his brothers still be able to record whether or not he was part of the group.

Branca renegotiated contracts with Epic Records. Michael had a contract as a solo artist and a separate contract as a member of The Jacksons. With Branca's help, Michael was able to secure the highest royalty rate in the music industry at that time. It was rumored that he received 37 percent of the wholesale price of his recordings.

At the Grammy Music Awards of 1980, Michael won his first Grammy for Best R&B Male Vocal Performance for "Don't Stop 'Til You Get Enough." Despite the high honor Michael was upset the album was not nominated for Album of the Year. According to an article in *Rolling Stone* magazine, the loss had "taught him a lesson. You could be the biggest black entertainer in history, and yet to much of the music industry and media, you were an invisible man."

Michael vowed to himself that he would never again go without earning the recognition he deserved. "My family thought I was going crazy because I was weeping so much about it. I felt ignored and it hurt. I said to myself, 'Wait until next time'—they won't be able to ignore the next album. That experience lit a fire in my soul."

It was during this period that Michael's appearance began to change. His use of plastic surgeons began because of an accident. In the spring of 1979, while rehearsing a complicated dance he tripped and fell, breaking his nose. To repair the damage, Michael underwent a procedure known as rhinoplasty. When the bandages were removed he was pleased to discover his nose was thinner. Perhaps now his brothers would no longer refer to him as "Big Nose."

Within the year, however, he developed breathing complications that interfered with his ability to sing. Michael elected to undergo another surgical procedure on his nose. The result after the second surgery convinced him that he no longer looked like his father. Friends and family complimented him on his new look, but few of them realized how obsessed Michael was becoming about perfection in all arenas of his life. Just as he might record a song two dozen times before being satisfied, time would prove that Michael would not be able to stop altering his appearance.

With this new look, Michael gained some confidence. This was evident in his sense of style—he knew wearing shortened trousers and white glittering socks was sure to draw attention. "Style is a mode of confrontation," he said.

Michael Jackson through the years.
From top left: 1971, 1977, 1979, and bottom: 1983, 1987, 1990 (Courtesy of AP Photo)

As Michael's solo career was taking off, his father was going through financial struggles. To Joseph's credit, he did not try to take money from his children's income to solve his latest financial troubles. In 1981 Michael helped his father by buying his Encino estate.

Joseph resisted the sale. He knew that if he allowed his twenty-three-year-old son to bail him out of his problems, the power struggle between the two of them would be altered. At first it was agreed that Michael would buy half the property, but soon Joseph was compelled to sell his quarter share of the place to Michael. This left Katherine with a quarter ownership. Now, if Katherine decided to kick Joseph out of their home again she would have the legal rights to do so. This was important to Michael. Years later, he would continue to reluctantly agree to various family financial projects, knowing that by helping Joseph out it would help his mother.

Michael was learning how to take command of his life. He demonstrated this by having the Encino house demolished so that a new ornate home could be built in its place. In the new home Michael's bedroom was large and eventually would include posters of Peter Pan, piles of books and records, and five female mannequins. Each mannequin was of a different race and looked like a high-fashion model. "I guess I want to bring them to life," he explained. "Being an entertainer, you just can't tell who is your friend. So, I surround myself with people I want to be my friends. And I can do that with mannequins. I'll talk to them."

His sister LaToya was among the family members who lived in this Tudor-styled house they had renamed "Hayvenhurst," the name of the street on which it was located. Her bedroom was so close to Michael's that she would complain that she could not sleep at night because her brother didn't sleep and had to find ways to stay entertained. She explained, "You hear music in his room when he's trying to create. Or you hear *The Three Stooges* on TV, and he's up all night laughing. The light is always on; Michael is forever reading books." Sundays at home were reserved for dancing. Often, this was what helped him get through bad times. Family members knew to not get in the way of Michael's need to dance on Sundays.

Michael was restless and constantly watched every detail around him. He was also becoming even more ambitious for his solo career. He was so dissatisfied with the recognition of his *Off the Wall* album that he was clearly distracted while performing with his brothers on stage. The family sensed that Michael was separating himself from them both on stage and off-stage. He was a perfectionist and had realized that he was best suited to be a solo performer where he could have more exacting control on his performance. The time was nearing for him to put together his creative energies. He decided to approach Quincy Jones to help him record another solo album that they would eventually name *Thriller.*

Chapter Five
Thriller

> " *I'm Michael Jackson.*
> *I make my own decisions.* "
> Michael Jackson

In 1982, Epic Records approved a budget of $750,000 to produce the next Michael Jackson album. Before entering the studio, Quincy Jones and Michael listened to and considered almost three hundred songs. They chose nine songs for the *Thriller* album. Listening to this many songs was not a common approach to producing an album, but Jones knew Michael believed in excellence. "I've worked with fifty-nine divas," Jones said. "All of them are complicated. When you are trying to make great art, you don't want the girl next door."

Michael had enjoyed his taste of creative control while producing *Off the Wall*. It had also given him a better idea of what he wanted his music to do. Contrary to the trend toward themed albums that was in style during the early 1980s, he wanted to produce an album without a cohesive theme.

He wanted songs that ranged from pop to soul to rock to funk. People in the industry were doubtful that this would work. In an interview with *Ebony* in 2007, Michael was still eager to explain his reasoning behind *Thriller*:

Ever since I was a little boy, I would study composition. And it was Tchaikovsky that influenced me the most. If you take an album like "Nutcracker Suite," every song is a killer, every one. So I said to myself, 'Why can't there be a pop album where every . . . —'people used to do an album where you'd get one good song and the rest were like B-sides. They'd call them "album songs"—and I would say to myself, 'Why can't every one be like a hit song? Why can't every song be so great that people would want to buy it if you could release it as a single?' So I always tried to strive for that. That was my purpose for the next album. That was the whole idea.

By August of 1982, Michael and Jones were in the Westlake Studio, listening to the final mix of the album. The final mix is also known as the master pressing. If this final version of the recordings is approved, the album is ready to be released to the public. But Michael was not pleased with what he heard on the final mix. It did not sound the way he had heard it in his head and he insisted on each song being remixed. This was a time-consuming process. Some voice lines would have to be toned down, some orchestrations would have to be brought up to a higher level. At the rate of remixing two songs each week, it was more than six weeks later before another final mix was ready to be heard.

Among the people in the room with Michael when he listened to the new final mix was Jones and Michael's attorney, Branca.

As the music played, Michael's smile indicated his approval. Jones and the studio crew were also pleased, but Jones cautioned Michael. He told him that the record market had been in a slump and that people were not buying music. It was Jones's opinion that perhaps the *Thriller* album would sell 2 million copies and if it could do so, it would be a hot album. Epic would be pleased with such sales.

Michael could not believe what he was hearing. He could not understand how Quincy Jones could be that wrong about the potential sales of this album. He was sure of himself and sure of where he stood with Epic Records and angry at what he saw as Jones's lack of confidence in his work. He left the studio and insisted that his attorney let Epic Records know that the record was canceled. If no one but Michael had faith that this album would outsell *Off the Wall*, then he wanted nothing to do with the team who had helped him produce it.

His years of working with an intimidating father and Berry Gordy at Motown had taught Michael how and when to stand up for himself and his musical instincts. When Epic Records received news from Branca that Michael was upset with their low expectations of how successful *Thriller* would be they were quick to soothe him. They told him that he was the superstar, and that he knew best how well the album would sell. They promised to press enough copies to keep up with demand. Appeased, Michael agreed to allow the album to be released.

Although his emotional outburst got him the attention and resolution he wanted this time, Michael's world was filling up with people unable to tell him "no." Later, this would not serve him well in both his personal and business life.

The first song released from the *Thriller* album was "The Girl Is Mine," featuring a duet with Paul McCartney, a former member of The Beatles. Some radio stations refused to play the song because of the interracial romance suggested in the lyrics, but the song was popular around the world, which helped Michael achieve worldwide recognition.

Shortly after "The Girl Is Mine" was released, the first of the four songs Michael wrote for the album, this one called "Billie Jean," hit the airwaves. Quincy Jones had not wanted the song on *Thriller.* Michael had felt otherwise, sensing that this song would be powerful.

After its release, there was much speculation among the public as to whether the song was based on a true event in Michael's life. The lyrics include lines about a baby an obsessed fan accused him of fathering. It was not uncommon for him to hear from fans claiming he had fathered their child, but this particular fan had gone so far as to send Michael a photo of herself and the baby, which of course had not been fathered by Michael. Also included in the package was a gun and a note asking Michael to kill himself on a set day, at a set time. For some time after that, he was more nervous than usual. A few years later he disavowed that this song was based on any real person, not wanting to encourage any more overly zealous fans.

He wrote another song, "Beat It," because he wanted to "write the type of rock song that I would go out and buy." On the album Michael leads the rhythm section by pounding out the rhythm on

Paul McCartney and Michael Jackson, 1982
(Courtesy of Giles Petard /Dalle/Landov)

boxes and crates scattered throughout the recording studio. In the album credits he is listed as "drum-case beater."

Michael had been right about most of his production demands. He was also right about the number that would be sold. The numbers were staggering. By the end of 1983 more than 22 million copies had been sold worldwide. (One month after Michael's death, *Thriller* sales would total more than 110 million copies.) The recording industry had been in a slump, as Jones had said, but due to the sales of *Thriller* Michael was given credit for single-handedly reviving a dormant industry and for uniting a varied audience. It was a rare achievement, but in years to come the album would become a psychological burden on Michael as he came to realize he'd never again achieve such success. He would spend the rest of his life determined to beat himself and outdo the success of this album.

At the height of this musical success, Michael found himself in a Motown

recording studio late one night. He had leased the studio in order to experiment with remixing a special edition of "Billie Jean." Focused on the control board, Michael was surprised to look up and see Berry Gordy in the room with him. As they listened to the tracks, Gordy asked Michael for a favor. Motown Records was planning a television special in celebration of its twenty-fifth anniversary. Gordy asked Michael to appear on the show with his brothers.

Michael no longer wanted to perform with his brothers. He told Gordy that if he agreed to do this for Motown he wanted a solo spot on the show as well. Gordy agreed, assuming Michael would perform one of his solos from his Motown days. But Michael said that if he were to sing on a Motown special, he would also need to perform an Epic Records song because that was the record company he was currently signed to.

After Gordy agreed to this Michael added one final stipulation. He was to do the final edit on the videotape of his solo before it was broadcast. This was a highly unusual request. Producers and directors normally maintain control on what they produce, but Michael had become such a huge star that Gordy agreed to extend editing rights to him. Michael explained, "Every shot is my shot. You're filming WHAT you want people to see, WHEN you want them to see it, HOW you want them to see it, what JUXTAPOSITION you want them to see. I know the emotion that I felt when I performed it, and I try to recapture that same emotion when I cut and edit and direct."

Often referred to as one of the most magical moments of his career, Michael Jackson's performance of "Billie Jean" on the "Motown 25th Anniversary Show" included a few seconds of his legendary dance, the moonwalk. The dance move was not new, but Michael had made the move famous. Although a backslide move, the moonwalk causes the dancer to appear as though he is moving backward while stepping forward. Michael refined his technique by studying and working out with an assortment of dancers, including self-taught street dancers such as Geron Candidate and Adolfo "Shabba Doo" Quinones, who was amazed that Michael would work himself to exhaustion in order to perfect the move.

Michael Jackson performing in the "Motown 25th Anniversary Show," 1983 *(Courtesy of Paul Drinkwater/NBCU Photo Bank/Associated Press)*

After the performance, Michael was initially upset with himself. He was more aware of what he could have done better than he was aware of what he had done well. This doubt was in despite of the reception he received backstage. Performers who he had listened to and watched as a little boy were stunned at how far he had developed. He was congratulated by Marvin Gaye, The Temptations, and Smokey Robinson. Richard Pryor, a famous African American comedian, told him the performance was the greatest he had ever seen. The following day Fred Astaire, the man often credited as being the best popular dancer of modern times, would call him at home to tell him that he was a "helluva mover." But it was the praise of a child that helped Michael realize he had given his greatest performance that night. A small boy dressed in a tuxedo approached Michael backstage and asked who taught him how to move like that. Michael replied, "I guess God . . . and rehearsal."

Michael decided to make a fourteen-minute video of the song "Thriller." He had just recently watched the movie *An American Werewolf in London* and was fascinated by the supernatural monsters in the movie. John Landis, the producer of that movie, recalled the evening Michael called him to ask him to produce his video and said, "I want to turn into a monster. Can I do that?" When he met with Michael to discuss the production, Landis showed up with a book filled with examples of monsters he could choose for his music video.

They had another idea as well. Why not make a video about the making of the *Thriller* video? This innovative marketing idea was the first of its kind in the world of music videos. Michael would also break new ground with a budget of more than $1.2 million for the mini-documentary *Making*

Michael Jackson's Thriller. It was the most expensive video ever created at that time.

Breaking new ground was what Michael thrived on, but what he hadn't counted on was the reaction to the video from the Jehovah's Witnesses church he attended. The church felt the video was evil because of its supernatural elements. A meeting with church leaders ended with Michael agreeing to include a written disclaimer at the beginning: "Due to my strong personal convictions, I wish to stress that this film in no way endorses a belief in the occult—Michael Jackson."

Each time he accomplished one goal, he would create a more difficult goal to tackle next. Breaking the unspoken racial barrier at MTV was important to Michael. When he and his brothers first watched the MTV channel, they were amazed that there could be music on television twenty-four hours a day. Michael's first love was performing on stage and soon he was determined to create the videos that MTV could not turn down. He told his brother Jackie, "If only they could give this stuff some more entertainment value, more story, a little more dance, I'm sure people would like it more. It's gotta have a story—an opening, a middle and a closing." This was what he had in mind when he created the *Thriller* music video.

Michael later recalled that when MTV said they didn't often play black artists, "It broke my heart, but at the same time it lit something." MTV was a rock and roll station when it began airing in 1981. Because, from their point-of view, most rock and roll artists were white, less than twenty videos featuring black performers had aired in the channel's first eighteen months on air. Another complication was that their research department felt that white suburban kids, the primary audience, wouldn't be interested in black music.

The "Billie Jean" video was initially rejected when Epic Records, which was owned by the powerful television network CBS, first submitted it to MTV for consideration. CBS insisted that MTV reconsider the video, suggesting that it would cancel all of its other videos unless MTV ran it. As a result, in early 1983, "Billie Jean" was broadcast on MTV.

For many who chartered the rise and fall of music stars, Michael Jackson had become unarguably the biggest star on the planet after his performance of "Billie Jean" on the Motown special. Once his "Thriller"

Michael Jackson posing in a scene from his "Thriller" music video *(Courtesy of Photos 12/Alamy)*

video was broadcast on MTV, it made him the icon of MTV and racial barriers were gone.

Michael's "Thriller" video was fashioned as a full-length movie condensed into fourteen minutes of spectacular dancing, special effects, and a plot complete with romance and suspense. Michael played the role of a boyfriend to a young pretty girl, asking her to go steady with him. When she agrees, he warns her that he isn't like other guys. As the music swells, Michael turns into a werecat. Werecats later turned into zombies in the video. Michael was challenged to choreograph the dancing werecats, monsters, and zombies so they would appear spooky and horrifying, but not comical. The results were horrifyingly successful. The elaborate care shown in the making of this video was instrumental in setting a new high mark for all future music videos. In 1999 MTV would hail it as the greatest music video ever made.

Chapter Six
One White Glove

> *It's a difficult life.*
> Michael Jackson

I n January 1984 Michael agreed to make two Pepsi-Cola commercials with his brothers. On the day of filming the concert commercial, more than 3,000 fans waited expectantly in the Los Angeles Shrine Auditorium for their role in simulating a live concert. The Jacksons were hustling around back stage with costume adjustments and final hair and makeup touches. The atmosphere was tense because every minute of preparation added thousands of dollars to the production costs. Bob Giraldi, the director, was anxious to get the cameras rolling. Suddenly Michael turned back from the stage, insisting he had to use the bathroom. "Use mine," Giraldi offered, because his bathroom was closer.

Everyone stood still, waiting. Seconds passed. More seconds passed, and then they heard an ear-splitting scream.

Giraldi panicked, thinking perhaps a crazy fan had hidden in the bathroom hoping to meet Michael. He raced to the bathroom and pounded on the door. The door slowly opened and when Giraldi and the crew rushed in Michael told them he had dropped his famous white rhinestone glove. "Where is it?" Giraldi wanted to know. Michael pointed to the toilet bowl. After a moment of disbelief, the crew rushed out of the small room in search of a coat hanger. Time was of the essence. Michael shrugged, reached into the toilet and retrieved the glove, and asked for a hair dryer.

The incident was soon forgotten when some time later, Michael descended a set of stairs on the concert stage, dancing and singing to his song "You're a Whole New Generation," which was based on the music from "Billie Jean." Then one of the most momentous, and tragic, events in Michael's life happened.

At first no one realized what was happening when Michael was suddenly in the middle of a cloud of smoke, but it quickly became obvious. As he danced, pyrotechnics were scheduled

Opposite Page: Michael, background, is seen with his hair on fire while Jermaine, foreground, apparently unaware of the situation, continues to perform. *(Courtesy of HO/AP Photo)*

to go off behind him to illuminate him in a silhouette. But something went wrong with the timing and Michael's hair and scalp caught on fire. At first no one realized how severe the injuries were, including Michael. As they rushed to Cedars-Sinai Medical Center, Michael, ever the consummate

The six Jackson brothers on the set of the 1984 Pepsi-Cola commercial. From far left to right: Tito, Jermaine, Jackie, Michael, Randy, and Marlon Jackson *(Courtesy of Associated Press)*

showman, had the presence of mind to insist he wear his glove as he was raced out of the auditorium on a stretcher.

With so many companies involved in the production of the much-heralded commercial, mass confusion ensued in determining who was at fault for Michael's accident. Michael had been hesitant to agree to be involved in the commercials to begin with because he did not care for the methods and integrity of the producer, Don King. While the painful accident resulted in worldwide sympathy and publicity for Michael, he would spend the remainder of his life dealing with pain and complications with his scalp. Many have speculated that Michael's eventual addiction to painkillers can be traced back to this event. When Pepsi-Cola agreed to pay him $1.5 million because of the accident, Michael, in his usual generous ways, donated the money to the Michael Jackson Burn Center.

Michael was twenty-five years old and understood business and public relations. What was beyond his control and understanding, though, was his family. The Jacksons insisted that they needed him on their *Victory* tour. He had just earned a record eight Grammy Awards, with "Beat It" winning the Record of the Year and *Thriller* winning the Best Album of the Year. With Michael on tour with them, The Jacksons were sure to have forty successful concert dates.

But Michael did not care for the way promoter Don King intended to produce the tour. King wanted all tickets sold by mail order, which exasperated Michael as well as his fans. Under King's proposal, more than 12 million fans would send in more than $1.5 billion in money orders in the hope of being one in ten applicants to actually receive the tickets. King's promise to return the money to fans who did not get tickets was met with growing suspicion, and eventually King agreed to allow fans to obtain tickets in the then usual manner of buying tickets at the box office.

Because Michael had his own attorney, his brothers retained their own attorneys. In the mix of this, Joseph Jackson was doing what he could to make sure no decisions could be made without his approval. Side meetings between brothers and attorneys were frequent and often psychologically damaging to the various Jacksons.

Michael refused to rehearse with his brothers on any *Victory* songs and as a result his brothers didn't perform any of their new songs on the tour. Jermaine was adamant that he perform three solos, and Michael was determined his solo hits be saved for the end of the concert. Michael referred to this tour as "The Final Curtain," which indicated this would be the last tour he did with The Jacksons. Too much had changed between them for the group to continue. The majority of the tickets were sold to Michael's fans, who hoped to see him perform the way they had seen him perform on the "Motown 25th Anniversary" television program. This inevitably meant his brothers would play supporting roles they were not comfortable with.

Tensions increased even more when they were approached with an offer to film the concerts so a film could be released afterward. Michael, however, had grown accustomed to his own high standard of creative control and knew he couldn't exert it on a joint project. He rejected the offer. This decision was difficult for his brothers, who would have made a great deal of money from the film, to accept.

As he grew wealthier, money seemed to be of little importance to Michael, but it revealed deep divisions in the Jackson family. During the concert tour they traveled in separate limousines and jets. Michael pledged to donate his portion of the tour income ($7 million) to charity. It was a not very subtle way of showing his family that his decisions and complaints about the way the tour was run had nothing to do with money. Michael's brothers felt he was a traitor to the family by not caring enough to put the family's interest ahead of his own.

Meanwhile, Michael had his attorney, Branca, check into the possibility of purchasing the publishing rights to a variety of available songs. Owning the publishing rights to a song or to any other intellectual property allows the owner to make decisions regarding when, where, and how the song will be used in various medias, including television, radio, movies, and advertisements. Royalties are also paid to the owner of the copyright and the owner of the publishing rights.

When he had worked with Paul McCartney in London on the song "Say, Say, Say," Michael became friends with Paul and his wife, Linda. At one point Paul showed him a file of the Buddy Holly songs he had bought. Although he had purchased the rights to these songs, he had never come up with enough money to purchase the rights to most of the songs he had written while with The Beatles. He and Yoko Ono, John Lennon's widow, had considered purchasing the publishing rights together, but determined that the price was too high and that it would be difficult to agree with each other as to what songs to release and for what reasons.

Michael was fascinated with the idea of buying up rights to songs. He saw it as a solid investment in a business he understood from the bottom up. Earlier, when he signed with Epic Records, he had made sure he owned the publishing rights to his own songs. It had been one of the reasons he and his family had left Motown.

When Branca called to tell him that after ten long grueling months of negotiations he had won the bid to purchase the ATV Music Publishing Company for $47.5 million, Michael was thrilled—and the world was shocked. This was said to be the biggest purchase of its kind in the music industry. Included in this purchase were 251 Beatles songs written from 1964 through 1971.

The Beatles, a four-man group from England, had become a sensation in the United States when they landed in New York City's Kennedy Airport on February 7, 1964. Their fourth British hit, "I Want to Hold Your Hand," had become their first number one hit in America, and young people were caught up in what was known as "Beatlemania." The band was widely merchandised with Beatles wigs, lunch boxes, and dolls, and was credited with opening the American door for other British groups such as the Rolling Stones and the Kinks. By 1965 The

Courtesy of Steven May/Alamy

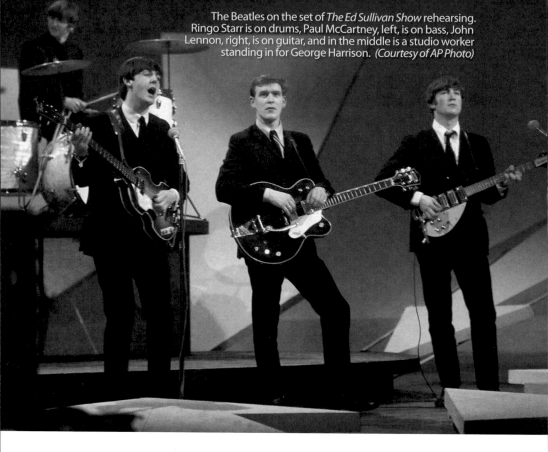

The Beatles on the set of *The Ed Sullivan Show* rehearsing. Ringo Starr is on drums, Paul McCartney, left, is on bass, John Lennon, right, is on guitar, and in the middle is a studio worker standing in for George Harrison. *(Courtesy of AP Photo)*

Beatles were considered, along with Bob Dylan, to be spokesmen for youth culture.

Caught up in their rapid rise to the top of the popular music world, John Lennon and Paul McCartney, the group's major songwriters, failed to learn enough about the business side of the music industry. Their biggest mistake was to not realize they should have kept the rights to the songs they wrote.

Michael's purchase of part of the Beatles' catalog was hurtful to Paul and Linda McCartney, although Yoko Ono, John Lennon's widow, was satisfied with the transaction. Now, any time Paul McCartney performed one of the songs he had written himself, he had to pay Michael Jackson a royalty fee. Michael Jackson, as publisher, also controlled the use of these songs in any films or commercials. Both Michael and Yoko Ono felt it was a good decision to allow Nike to use the song "Revolution" to promote their products, but Paul felt it cheapened the Beatles' legacy. Similar decisions would continue to bother Paul.

As the Jackson's *Victory* tour came to an end, Michael was approached to help on a project sponsored by the USA in Africa fund designed to help feed the hungry population in Ethiopia. The project would earn $8 million for the fund and Michael was eager to participate. He spoke about the despair he felt when he realized that it was impossible for political entities to cure all the troubles in the world: "It's beyond us. Look, we don't have control over the grounds, they can shake. We don't have control over the seas, they can have tsunamis. We're all in God's hands. I just wish they would do more for the babies and children, help them more. That would be great, wouldn't it?"

Harry Belafonte, an acclaimed songwriter and singer, wanted to bring together the biggest musical artists in the country for a recording of a song entitled "We Are the World." Lionel Richie, another popular artist at the time, was asked to write the song. Lionel asked Michael if he would like to help. Ever the perfectionist, Michael worked with Lionel every night for a week.

As they were composing the song, Belafonte recruited an all-star cast that included Bruce Springsteen, Tina Turner, Stevie Wonder, Willie Nelson, Bob Dylan, Ray Charles, Billy Joel, Bette Midler, and Diana Ross. All told, forty-five artists showed up to record the song on the night of the American Music Awards. As each performer entered the recording studio after the AMA show was over, they were greeted with a sign that stated, "Please check your egos at the door."

The only invited artist who failed to show was Prince. Prince, as shy as Michael, found the idea of recording with so many artists at the same time to be emotionally overwhelming. His offer to later record a guitar track for the song was turned down. His album *Purple Rain* had recently been released and was driving Prince to superstardom. He would win the 1985 Grammy Award for Best Group Rock Vocal. Frequently compared to Michael and Madonna, Prince was known for his dancing and singing. He was also accomplished at composing, producing, and playing all the instruments on his first five albums.

Michael had become an integral part of the production, which also included a video, but he refused to record his section of the song with the gathered artists. His solo was taped later and, as was now customary anytime Michael was filmed, he controlled the camera work. It was his idea to promote himself in all films by having his sequined white socks videoed first, then his solo glove and then, for just a few seconds, his face was revealed. He understood the power of a "brand." Quincy Jones, also involved in the production of "We Are The World," was accustomed to Michael's extreme perfectionism and self-appointed isolationism, but for most of the others involved in this project this experience with such a shy man was new to them.

Michael had been isolated in his childhood. His mother's Jehovah's Witnesses's belief system had scorned much of the community. He was even more isolated by becoming a major singing star at such a young age. As an adult, being isolated had become such a way of life that he avoided most people.

Some of the artists calling themselves "USA for Africa" recording "We Are The World" in L.A., 1985. *(Courtesy of AP Photo)*

Entanglements with others were simply too difficult. He couldn't do normal things in public like go grocery shopping or visit a library. It wasn't possible to go shopping for himself because he would get mobbed by fans. He explained, "You don't get peace in a shop. If they don't know your name, they know your voice. And you can't hide."

Michael could best identify with other people who had been childhood stars. He befriended Brooke Shields, Liza Minnelli, and Elizabeth Taylor, who had all been famous as children. They remained friends with him his entire life, and were capable of understanding Michael's shyness and remoteness.

It was Jane Fonda, a famous actress and daughter to another famous actor, Henry Fonda, who first mentioned to Michael that he was like Peter Pan. Peter Pan lived on an island known as Never Never Land in the children's story about a boy who refused to grow up. She pointed out he also surrounded himself with strong women as a way of finding his own inner strength. "In some ways," she recalled, "Michael reminded me of the walking wounded, an extremely fragile person."

Michael continued to undergo more plastic surgery. He told people that knowing he had a choice about what his face looked like was one of the best things he had ever experienced in his life. Some people speculated that Michael wanted to look like Diana Ross with thin eyebrows, exacting makeup, and a tapered nose. Diana Ross represented his idea of physical perfection. As his appearance changed over the years, Michael became what many called "a self-created piece of art."

Others speculated Michael underwent so much plastic surgery in order to distance himself from resembling his father, Joseph. While Michael demonstrated at an early age that he had his father's almost ruthless determination and cold-hearted business sense, he might have thought that the less he was like his father on the outside, the less he might be like him on the inside. Whatever the reasons for his growing need for plastic surgery were, in June of 1986 Michael had his fourth rhinoplasty and arranged to have a cleft cut into his chin.

Chapter Seven
Who Is the Man in the Mirror?

They called Elvis The King.
Why don't they call me that?
Michael Jackson

aped to a mirror in Michael's black and gold bathroom, above the faucets shaped like golden swans, was a note he had written to himself: "100 million." By 1986 it had been four years since the release of *Thriller* and he was desperate to produce an album that would top it by selling 100 million copies.

When Michael recorded in the studio, he had the lights turned off. As he sang he danced on a wooden stage he had built. Although Michael could not read music, he either memorized his songs or sang them into a tape recorder. Later, he would hire musicians to write them down. When asked about the inspiration for the songs he wrote Michael explained, "I wake up from dreams and go, 'Wow, put *this* down on paper. The whole thing is strange. You hear the words, everything is right there in front of your face. And you say to yourself, 'I'm sorry, I just didn't write this. It's there already.' I'm just a courier bringing it into the world. I'm happy at what I do. It's escapism."

By August 1986, he had written more than sixty songs for he and Quincy to consider for the next album, which would be called *Bad*. They painstakingly selected eight and then found two more songs from other songwriters.

Bad took more than two years to complete and cost more than $2 million. Finally, his manager and lawyer insisted that it be completed by June 30, 1987, because a tour of Japan was scheduled to begin in September and they needed an album to present in conjunction with the tour. Finally, Michael reluctantly agreed to allow *Bad* to be released. His manager explained, "The closer he gets to completing it, the more terrified he becomes of that confrontation with the public."

Commercially, the work paid off. The *Bad* album would go on to sell more than 32 million copies and produced five number one songs, including "Man in the Mirror." But this major success was not enough for Michael. It had not done better than *Thriller*. Also, many of his fellow musicians considered it to be a letdown that failed to capture the excitement the earlier record had created. Michael was hurt by the criticism. Stevie Wonder, a highly acclaimed singer and songwriter who had also got his start at Motown, had sung a duet with him on "Just Good Friends." Wonder warned Michael that "you can't think about what people will like; you go crazy doing that." Quincy Jones often told people that Michael was "the oldest man I know, and he's the youngest kid I know."

He might have been childlike in some of his characteristics and emotions, but Michael was a genius at public relations.

Michael's album *Bad*
(Courtesy of Felix Hoerhager/dpa /Landov)

He decided to focus on creating the "greatest show on earth." He took the slogan from the famous circus promoter P. T. Barnum, whose biography was one of his favorite books. He had given a copy of the book to his manager Frank Dileo and John Branca, his attorney, telling them that this was the model of public relations and business he wanted to use for the promotion of himself.

During this time period, Michael had also just completed the filming of *Captain EO*. This seventeen-minute video was one of the most expensive music videos ever produced, costing an estimated $20 million. In order for it to premiere at both the Epcot Center and Disney World in Orlando, Florida, and Disneyland in Anaheim, California, both parks built theaters that could accommodate tilting floors and smoke coming out of the screen.

To promote the video, Michael wanted to come up with a gimmick that would gain him worldwide attention. Two years earlier, when he was being treated for his burns from the Pepsi commercial, he had the opportunity to see a special oxygen chamber at Brotman Memorial Hospital. Designed to surround the patient with 100 percent oxygen with an increased barometric pressure, the chamber was shaped like a casket. This treatment, known as hyperbaric therapy, required the attendance of trained medical personnel in order to ensure the safe use of the chamber. Theories about the chamber included that it could prolong one's life. Michael was fascinated.

Promotional poster for *Captain EO*

In a clever use of the media, Michael was able to get the *National Enquirer*, a newspaper well-known for publishing sensationalized stories, to run a photo of him in the chamber. Every major press outlet in the country ran the story afterward. As a result, Michael's name was on the front page of most prominent newspapers. His manager further fueled the drama by interviewing with a variety of national magazines, vowing that he would not allow Michael to buy the chamber for his own use.

Michael marveled at his success in creating a media buzz. "We can actually *control* the press," he said. In his mind, this was not only a publicity stunt to gather attention for his *Captain EO* video, but also a joke played against an enemy. He did not trust the media and rarely granted interviews, and he found it satisfying to trick newspapers and magazines into publicizing something that was not true. Charles Montgomery, who worked for the *National Enquirer* at the time, spoke of Michael's business instincts. "Michael is one of the smartest entertainers in the business. He knows how to get his name out there. He knows about PR [public relations]. He knows how to control his career. I think he's brilliant."

Michael engineered another stunt regarding the Elephant Man's bones. In 1980 a movie had been made, starring John Hurt, that was based on the life of John Merrick, who had been born deformed and became a famous carnival attraction in the nineteenth century. When he passed away, Merrick's bones were preserved at the London Hospital Medical College. Michael made a show of insisting that he be allowed to purchase the bones and have them moved into his home. While this never came to pass, the media had quite a time with the oddity of such a request.

Another media speculation was that Michael wanted to learn to talk "monkey language" in order to better communicate with Bubbles, a three-year-old chimpanzee he had made into a pet after it was released from a cancer lab in 1985. Owning Bubbles was not a stunt. Michael owned numerous exotic pets, but the story of wanting to talk "monkey language" was a fabrication.

Unfortunately, there were unintended consequences of these promotional ideas. As a result of the oxygen chamber and elephant man bones rumors, the public began to reconsider him. In Britain, the tabloids dubbed him "Wacko Jacko," an offensive nickname he would never live down.

The elders at his Jehovah's Witnesses church in Woodland, California, were also following the bizarre media stunts. Not for the first time did they take Michael to task for his choices and behavior. It was felt that his lifestyle and creative expression in his work was contrary to what they believed. As the tension increased, Michael made the decision to permanently leave the church.

The fallout from this period of publicity stunts would be a burden to Michael the rest of his life. As he continued to struggle at topping his *Thriller* success, he began to feel that many people, even former fans, were heartless towards him and critical of both his creative and humanitarian endeavors. He became known instead as eccentric, reclusive, and a person to whom few people wanted to relate. At one point, Michael wrote a letter to the editor of *People* magazine, a prominent newsstand magazine with one of the highest circulations in the world. In the open letter, Michael asked that he not be judged. He reminded everyone that he lived for the children all over the world and that when wrongful things were said about him it also hurt the children.

Added to this pressure was a new musical competitor, his baby sister Janet. Janet had shot to the top of the pop music charts while Michael was struggling with the production of *Bad*. She had recorded her first two albums with her father acting as her production manager, and both albums had been unsuccessful. In 1986, she began work on her next album, *Control*, after dropping her father and realigning herself with a younger records executive, John McClain.

McClain brought in new songwriters, Jimmy Jam and Terry Lewis, and sent Janet to Canyon Ranch in Arizona, a health spa, to lose weight and to get into top physical shape. Then he had her work on her dance moves with the highly acclaimed choreographer Paula Abdul. All the work paid off. Her new album became one of the ten best-selling albums of 1986.

Janet would go on to be named one of Billboard's Top Ten Best-Selling Artists in the history of contemporary music. She always said that of all her brothers she was closest to Michael. "Out of everyone in the family, we're the two that think the most alike," she said. Michael, however, was not used to sharing the attention. He had always been the star in the family.

1989 photograph of Janet
(Courtesy of Pictorial Press Ltd /Alamy)

Now he had a competitor. Soon Michael would only practice his dancing when Janet was not around. He didn't want her to learn anything from him.

For Michael, music was more about commercial success than about artistic expression. He measured his success by the number of albums sold, the number of sold-out concerts on a tour, and by the number of hit singles. Because of this focus on sales, some music critics felt that in the end he was limited as an artist. While some artists, such as Bruce Springsteen, Stevie Wonder, and Bob Dylan, seemed to be willing to go where their music took them without as much regard for how it sold, Michael was fenced in by the business of music. Other critics felt that even after Michael left Motown, he had never ceased to carry out Berry Gordy's model of creating black pop music that all demographics could enjoy without being challenged. Fairly or unfairly, this criticism stuck and hounded him throughout his career.

Other critics, however, found his stage performances unsurpassed. Michael's quick and precise moves were modeled after James Brown. Brown, often referred to as "The Godfather of Soul," was an influential singer and dancer in the late 1950s and 1960s best known for his feverish dance moves and uncanny rhythms. In addition to Brown's influence on Michael's performance, Michael incorporated mime in his style.

However, his inaccessibility to the media and increasing reputation for "weirdness" was taking a toll on Michael's popularity. In 1988 *Rolling Stone* magazine conducted its annual readers poll. Michael was voted the worst artist in almost every category. Although actress Elizabeth Taylor had suggested he was the "King of Pop," this designation did not set well with everyone.

Despite this negative readers' poll, Michael attended the Grammy Awards that year confident that he would win at least one of the four nominations accorded to his album, *Bad*. But he sat through the evening without recognition. The Grammy for the Best Album was awarded to U2 for *The Joshua Tree*.

The following day, after performing at Madison Square Garden, Michael presented a check to the United Negro College Fund for $600,000, adding to the scholarship program

Michael performing on his *Bad* tour at the Los Angeles Sports Arena, 1988
(Courtesy of Alan Greth/AP Photo)

that he had started some years earlier after the *Victory* tour. This generous side to Michael's personality was something he did not often publicize. While public attention was focused on his bizarre stunts, he was quietly donating all the royalties from his song "Man in the Mirror" to a charity for terminally ill patients in Los Angeles known as Camp Good Times.

In the spring of 1988, a Korean businessman approached the Jackson family with an offer to promote a Jackson family concert tour in Korea. In order to convince the Jacksons to consider the offer, no expenses were spared. Joseph and Katherine were flown to Korea and treated to a four-day tour of the country. If the Jacksons could get Michael to appear in the Korean tour, the Korean businessman would agree to invest $2 million in a record company for Michael's father. The man behind this plan was the Reverend Sun Myung Moon, who led a highly controversial religious movement many considered to be a cult.

As time went on, other members of the Jackson family were approached with offers of large amounts of money and expensive gifts if they could get Michael to agree to the tour. Initially, Michael refused the offer and became suspicious of his family. In the end, however, he gave in. "These people are going to drive me crazy until they get what they want. So, let's just do the shows and get it over with," he remarked. This philosophy of giving in to demands in hope that the conflict would dissipate was an approach that Michael had begun to adopt—but only after he had fired many of his top advisers who had previously handled all of Michael's affairs and would have refused to allow him to make the trip. In time Michael would learn that giving in to the wishes of others often did not turn out well.

Chapter Eight
Neverland

My guests expect something big. It's gotta look like I've made it big, because I have.
Michael Jackson

John Landis, who worked with Michael on the *Thriller* video among others, once commented: "With Michael, as with any superstar, reality and fantasy are totally confused. It's very difficult to remain sane."

In an attempt to gain complete control over his private and business life, Michael ceased working with Quincy Jones, who had produced *Off the Wall*, *Thriller*, and *Bad*. He thought Jones got too much credit for his success and controlled him too much in the recording studio. Michael also fired the man the music industry credited for his increased sales promotions, Frank Dileo. John Branca would also be replaced, only to be rehired later.

Michael decided to separate himself from his family at Hayvenhurst. He wanted a place where he could be alone.

He also wanted something big and grandiose enough to show to everyone that he was a major star—truly the "King of Pop." He had long envied Paul McCartney's vast property in England.

One of the places he considered buying was the Sycamore Ranch, where he and Paul had once stayed while recording. The ranch, located in the Santa Ynez Valley in California, had a main house of more than 13,000 square feet and was filled with more than $2.5 million worth of antique furnishings.

Michael's house on Neverland Ranch, 2003
(Courtesy of dpa/Landov)

It also included 2,700 acres. Negotiations for the purchase were carried out by John Branca and were kept secret from Michael's family.

After he took over ownership of the estate, it was Michael's plan to have his employees go to Hayvenhurst and remove his belongings and take them to his new home. He had no intention of talking to his family about the move ahead of time. He was afraid they would pressure him not to purchase the ranch.

His family learned of the purchase one evening while watching *Entertainment Tonight* on television.

Michael renamed the ranch Neverland Valley. Here he was finally able to create his own Magic Kingdom, one protected by armed guards around the clock. Stapled to the walls inside the guard post to the entrance of Neverland was a collection of photos of people who were potential threats. Each photo had a caption explaining why the person should be feared: "Might be armed," "Has been loitering near the gate," or "Believes she is married to Mr. Jackson." Stationed throughout the property were uniformed security guards, some standing at attention and others patrolling the grounds with the use of golf carts. In addition, there were thirty full-time gardeners and at least ten ranch hands to take care of the animals. One day, when standing in front of his three-story Tudor-styled home, Michael realized he owned all the land for as far as he could see.

He was determined to make his new home a fantasyland, a place that fulfilled his wildest dreams of what a perfect home should be. He built an amusement-park-style train that could hold more than twenty passengers to tour the grounds. The grounds also included a sizable lake, an Indian tepee village, a two-story fort, a carousel, a Ferris wheel, and a three-story slide.

Michael's animal collection, including three giraffes, were kept in his own zoo.

Neverland was created from a child's point of view. He wanted a place that children would want to visit. A $2 million theater was constructed so that guests could watch movies at any hour of the day or night. Next to it was a two-story rec-

Michael riding the carousel with some of his guests at Neverland Ranch, 1994 (Courtesy of AP Photo)

reation building with every sort of electronic game available. "Neverland isn't about kids going to sleep at a certain time. The kids really run the place when they're here," explained Lee Tucker, who helped design the theater complex.

Busloads of underprivileged and terminally ill children regularly visited. Any feature that could be added to the property

that would enhance the experience of a child was a feature Michael would readily agree to spend money to build.

One friend who was able to understand Michael's need for such a fantasyland was Elizabeth Taylor. A famous child star decades earlier, she, too, had been denied any resemblance of a childhood and had been raised by an abusive father. Their friendship had started when Michael had arranged to give her fourteen tickets to his *Thriller* concert. Taylor showed up at the concert with her friends, but was dismayed that her seats were in a box too far from the stage. She refused the seats and left with her group of friends.

When Michael learned of this after the concert, he called her in tears. She explained that she was accustomed to the best seats in the house. What might have ended most conversations right then and there instead resulted in a deep friendship that would last their lifetimes. When asked once how she felt about Michael's eccentricity she replied, "There's a vulnerability inside him which makes him the more dear. He is magic. And I think all truly magical people have to have that genuine eccentricity."

Michael was not at Neverland for most of the first three years he owned it. Much of his time was spent in recording studios and preparing for the release of his 1991 album, *Dangerous.* He wanted to come up with an album that had more of a "street feel" than his earlier music.

Realizing that the *Thriller* video helped sell more *Thriller* albums, Michael decided that a music video from the *Dangerous* album would be released first. It was estimated that more than half a billion people viewed the premiere of the video entitled "Black or White." On November 11, 1991, MTV, in return for the right to be the first to air the video, agreed to send a memo to all personnel that from that moment forward Michael Jackson was to be referred to as the "King of Pop."

If critics felt that Michael's music didn't take enough risks, they couldn't say the same about this video. In the highly controversial last four minutes, Michael simulated masturbation. Other parts of the video were violent. What was most upsetting, John Landis later speculated, was, "the juxtaposition of sex with the violence of smashing car windows and tossing a garbage can through a store window."

By this time, Michael had several child star friends. It was common for television and movie stars such as Emmanuel Lewis and Macaulay Culkin to be at Neverland. He also had friends from other walks of life. John Landis recalled later that his crew was all set to film on location when he happened to glance over to where he had several seven-foot tall speakers set up to play the song. Standing right in front of these speakers was none other than Nancy Reagan, the country's former First Lady.

The video "Black or White" stirred new debate about Michael's physical appearance. He was rarely seen when he wasn't wearing a surgical mask. Although he said it was to hide his identity, the true reason was because of damage to his nose. After too many surgeries, the tip of his nose no longer had any cartilage and he had to wear a latex appliance camouflaged with stage makeup. He could have worn a prosthesis, but that would involve a painstaking and painful procedure.

The changing color of his skin drew more public scrutiny and debate. Most sources confirmed that Michael had bleached his skin with a variety of chemicals. The continual use of these chemicals results in the skin being hypersensitive to sunlight. The medical community continues to debate whether or not such use can result in a skin disease known as vitiligo, from which Michael suffered.

In the late 1980s Michael's dermatologist diagnosed him with an autoimmune disease known as discoid lupus on his scalp, which might have been a consequence of the accident he had suffered while filming the Pepsi-Cola commercial years before. Treatment for this disease involved undergoing steroid injections directly into his scalp. A painful procedure, this was later considered to be one of the reasons Michael became addicted to painkillers.

The subject of Michael's skin color was defended by those who had worked with him on the *Dangerous* album. When Michael was accused of trying to make his skin more white, producer Terry Riley pointed out that if Michael had been ashamed of being African American he would not have contributed so much time and money on aid projects for Africa. He also pointed out that Michael's music stayed rooted in the rhythm and blues genre that he had learned as a young boy. Riley further noted, "Of course he loved being black. We'd be in sessions where we'd just vibe out. I know this man loved his culture, he loved his race, he loved his people."

Michael spent over twenty-five years trying in vain to outdo *Thriller* but he was probably fighting timing. *Thriller* had been the right album at the right time, and trying to make an album based on the same model failed to take into consideration some of the changes the society had undergone in the years since. He also faced new competition from new forms of music. A new style of music called rap was sweeping across the nation. Rock music, after dropping in popularity for a few years, was making a strong comeback in the early 1990s. In addition, other artists, such as Madonna, MC Hammer, and several other artists, were performing in a style very much like his. With *Dangerous*, Michael played it safe by producing an album that was much like his previous albums even though fans wanted something new.

Another pressure came from new technology, which made it all but impossible to achieve the same level of commercial success he had enjoyed with *Thriller*. In the early 1980s there was no World Wide Web or other formats for the mass public to select their own music. In the late 1990s a Boston college student, Shawn Fanning, developed Napster, an online music service that relied on individuals sharing their music files with each other. The music industry struggled to catch up with this new concept, claiming that such file sharing was a form of copyright violations. Though the industry would eventually win their case against Napster, album sales were dropping because of the new ways audiences had of obtaining music without paying for it. It seems unlikely any album could ever earn the revenues *Thriller* earned.

Although slower to develop, the same changes affected music videos. For several years MTV and a few other cable channels determined which music video was put on the air. Then, in early 2005, three former PayPal employees would create a site known as YouTube. Now every music artist would have to compete with thousands and thousands of other videos, making it nearly impossible for any one star to capture the market. With the nearly infinite menu of options available to music consumers it was almost impossible for any artist to gain the dominance that Michael and other artists, such as The Beatles, had had. However, Michael, along with many others in the music industry, would not realize how much things had changed for years.

Michael's last major musical impact was probably in 1993 when he agreed to a half time Super Bowl performance at the Rose Bowl stadium. He stunned viewers with a three-song medley.

As it would turn out, this would be the last of Michael's superstar moments. The rest of his life would be filled with controversy, embarrassment, and wrenching heartbreak.

Michael performing during halftime at
Super Bowl XXVII on January 31, 1993
(Courtesy of NFL Photos/AP Photo)

Chapter Nine
Marriage, Children, and $20 Million

Michael has a lot of people around him, but he's very afraid. I think it comes from his early days.

Diana Ross

By the early 1990s, Michael Jackson seemed to prefer to spend his time with children. Some people, including family and friends, thought it was odd. Michael, however, said that when he was with children he was able to experience some of the feel of the childhood he had missed out on when he was a child himself. He did not feel judged when he was with young children and explained, "Children know a lot of secrets and it is difficult to get them to tell. My most creative moments have almost always come when I am with children. When I am with them, the music comes to me as easily as breathing."

One day in 1992 Michael's jeep broke down on a busy street in Beverly Hills and no one would stop to help him, perhaps because he was dressed in his usual disguise of a black turban and black veil over his face. When he called a tow truck the driver was surprised to discover he had come to the aid of Michael Jackson. He called ahead to his office to inform his friends that he was bringing Michael Jackson back to the shop with him.

Once at the shop, Michael was thankful for the help and was pleased to meet the tow truck driver's friends and family. Among those there to meet him was a family with two children, a son and a daughter. He invited them to visit Neverland when he had a break from the upcoming tour to promote his new album, *Dangerous*.

The tour was extensive, beginning in Germany and winding its way throughout Europe and Eastern Asia. Two large cargo planes traveled with him. Included in the cargo were full-size video arcade games. During his long hours traveling or waiting in hotel rooms Michael would call the family, often discussing video games with their thirteen-year-old son.

In the first months of 1993, Michael returned to the United States in order to perform at President Clinton's Inaugural Ball, as well as the American Music Awards, the Super Bowl, and the NAACP Image Awards. He also agreed to do a television interview with Oprah Winfrey while her film crew gave an on-the-air tour of Neverland. During the interview, Elizabeth Taylor surprised the crew by showing up long enough to tell Oprah that Michael was "the least weird man I have ever known."

After the series of television appearances more than 210 million viewers had watched Michael on television in the span of a few weeks. He had also traveled thousands of miles on his tour. He was exhausted and needed a break. He called his new friends and invited the family to spend a weekend in Neverland.

This family was swept away by Michael's kindness. Mother, daughter, and son were treated to a private shopping spree at a toy store, something Michael often arranged for children visiting Neverland. The two children were informed that they could have whatever they wanted in the store. Brother and

Oprah Winfrey on a tour of Michael's estate during the taping of a live interview on February 10, 1993 *(Courtesy of Sam Emerson/Reuters/Landov)*

sister raced around the store filling shopping carts with more than $10,000 worth of toys.

This was only the first of several visits the family made to Neverland. Sometimes the visits with the family took place at Michael's condo, about ten minutes away from where the family lived. Other visits were away from California, including a weekend in Las Vegas in Michael's private suite at the Mirage Hotel. However, when Michael invited the family to go on tour with him the children's divorced father refused permission. He said he had become wary of Michael's influence on his son and his ex-wife.

As the boy's parents fought over the visits to Neverland the father decided to take matters into his own hands. Although one of the parents was always present during the visits, the young boy's father hired a lawyer to present Michael with an ultimatum. Either Michael could pay him $20 million or he would accuse Michael of child molestation. When Michael and his lawyers refused to negotiate, the Los Angeles Police Department began a criminal investigation of Michael based on the charges presented to them by the young boy's father.

Michael cut short his *Dangerous* tour and returned to deal with the police investigation. After four tense months, LAPD determined there was no evidence to support bringing

Anthony Pellicano, a private investigator for entertainer Michael Jackson, speaks to reporters during a brief news conference at the office of lawyer Howard Weitzman, right, in the Century City section of Los Angeles, on August 24, 1993. *(Courtesy of Nick Ut/AP Photo)*

criminal charges. At the same time, Michael agreed to an out-of-court settlement with the father of more than $20 million. Michael and his attorneys hoped that this would put an end to the nightmare. He did not seem to realize that paying the money would come to appear to be an admission of guilt to most people.

There was another reason Michael wanted to put the entire experience behind him. He had asked Lisa Marie Presley, the only child of the late "King of Rock and Roll" Elvis Presley, to marry him.

If anyone could understand Michael's peculiar lifestyle, it was Lisa Presley. Born on February 1, 1968, Lisa had been showered with gifts by her father. When she was five years old he presented her with a set of expensive jewels and her first fur coat. Odd behavior was customary in Graceland. Her father once shot the family's TV with a rifle when he didn't like what was on. Tragically, Elvis was struggling with drug addiction. Lisa was not yet ten when Elvis died from a massive drug overdose.

In 1993, Lisa and Michael were each invited to attend a private dinner at the home of a mutual friend. At the time Lisa was hoping to pursue a career in music but was wary of the recording industry, which she thought had mistreated her father. She was also afraid the world would compare her to her father and that she would inevitably not live up to the standard.

Talking with Michael boosted her confidence and self-esteem. Michael was drawn to her strong and emotionally open ways. The two of them soon formed a deep and intimate relationship.

As others had discovered, Michael was at his best when talking on the phone. Without the face-to-face interaction, he would open up and share his innermost thoughts. Lisa soon became his closest friend. Knowing both her father's fight with addiction and her own past struggle with drugs, Lisa felt she could make a difference in Michael's life and help him in his private battle with his abuse of prescription drugs. She remembered, "I started falling for him. I wanted to save him. I felt that I could do it."

Michael canceled the rest of the *Dangerous* tour after performing in Mexico City. Instead of flying back to California, he flew to London, where, under the guidance of both Lisa and Elizabeth Taylor, he had agreed to enter the Charter Nightingale Clinic for treatment. In a public statement he blamed past surgeries and the subsequent painkiller medications for his addiction. His family and his closest friends supported his decision, hoping treatment would give him a new perspective on life. During his rehabilitation therapy, Michael learned to quit blaming others (his father, the media, his lawyers) for what was wrong in his life. "I need to start over again," he said. "I want my life back."

The Jackson family was mostly supportive during this difficult time, but his sister LaToya shocked both family and friends in late 1993 with a press conference arranged by her husband, Jack. In her speech, she announced to the world that her brother, Michael Jackson, was a pedophile. The Jackson family was outraged and shocked, claiming that LaToya had been brainwashed by her greedy husband. For some weeks, LaToya's allegations made headline news across the world. On December 22, 1993, she agreed to appear on a television show based out of Madrid. She would restate her allegations regarding her brother, but this time while wired to a lie-detector machine.

Minutes before LaToya was to go on air, CNN broadcast a four-minute speech from Michael. Michael pleaded with everyone to be patient and not be quick to judge him. "I ask all of you to wait and hear the truth before you condemn me. Don't treat me like a criminal, because I am innocent." Sitting in a dressing room near the sound stage where she was to appear, LaToya watched the broadcast with tears in her eyes. Her husband, watching her, suddenly called off her appearance on the show. He insisted that unless the television producers would agree to double the $50,000 fee LaToya had been offered for her testimony he wouldn't let her appear. When the producers declined to double the payment he took LaToya by her arm and marched her off the sound stage. Years later, LaToya would admit that she had invented these allegations and that they had been masterminded by her husband, Jack. Not until 2003, ten years later, though, would Michael and LaToya make amends.

In May 1994, during a quiet ceremony in the Dominican Republic, Michael Jackson married Lisa Marie Presley, twenty days after Lisa's divorce from her first husband was final. Lisa's mother, Priscilla Presley, and Michael's family were not immediately informed about the wedding. Most of the world, in fact, did not learn of the marriage until months had passed. Michael enjoyed the secrecy and the games necessary to keep their marriage private. Once the marriage was made public, the general outcry was one of disbelief. People wondered why Lisa married him. She later admitted, "I actually did fall in love with him, but I didn't know what was on his menu."

Both Michael and Lisa were headstrong and accustomed to getting their way in every aspect of their lives. Lisa was determined to keep her own one-acre estate, located one hundred miles away from Neverland. As a practicing member of the Church of Scientology, Lisa felt her religion helped her take responsibility for her actions. It had been her hope that Michael would learn from this and perhaps become a scientologist and stop thinking of himself as a victim.

In June 1995, the couple agreed to be interviewed by Diane Sawyer. As unusual as it was for Michael to agree to a television interview, it was even more unusual for his wife. Lisa was a private but honest person and did not care to practice diplomacy in front of the cameras. She agreed to the show because she knew it was a good opportunity for the world to see the Michael Jackson she knew and loved. When Diane Sawyer asked the pressing question about why Michael would allow kids to sleep in his bed, Lisa defended Michael and confirmed that she felt Michael's interest in children was entirely innocent. When Diane asked Michael if he would quit having sleepovers at his house, he said no. He replied that kids could still continue to sleep over, "if they want. It's on the level of purity and love and just innocence, complete innocence."

Michael was adamant that he wanted children with Lisa. The longer they were together, the more impatient he became for Lisa to become pregnant. For Lisa, time spent with Michael was becoming difficult. He was often uncommunicative. At times, she would go for weeks without knowing where he was. When she accused him of being selfish with his time, he could not understand what she meant. As far as he was concerned, he couldn't be considered selfish if he was donating as much money as he donated to so many unfortunate children of the world.

One day at breakfast, Michael calmly mentioned that perhaps he would have a baby with the nurse from his

Michael and Lisa Marie at the 11th Annual MTV Music Video Awards at New York's Radio City Music Hall in 1994 *(Courtesy of Bebeto Matthews/AP Photo)*

dermatologist office. By this point in the marriage, Lisa was accustomed to Michael's odd and disjointed ideas. She told him that maybe that would be a good idea, but in fact she was startled and dismayed. She had no idea that Michael was friends with a nurse at the dermatologist's office. Eventually, she learned that Michael and Debbie Rowe had been friends for almost ten years.

Debbie had come to know Michael throughout the years of treatments he received from Dr. Arnold Klein. They became good friends, often talking into the morning on the telephone. She found him to be sweet and vulnerable, not at all like the strange man who was often in the news. Michael sent her gifts and autographed first copies of all his albums, which she framed and hung on the walls in her small home. When Michael was under stress, he knew he could call Debbie and calm down.

Lisa realized that she could not maintain her own steady focus on life while married to Michael. She filed for divorce in January 1996, one month after Michael had been hospitalized for yet another panic attack during a rehearsal for a concert at the Beacon Theater in New York. In March 1996, Debbie Rowe suffered a miscarriage. She claimed the baby had been Michael's. Life for Michael was growing more lonely. He was thirty-eight years old and felt that the only thing that hadn't failed him was his own determination. Now he had decided to become a father and was determined nothing would get in the way of that goal.

Chapter Ten
HIStory

Why does everyone else get to be happy, and I'm always thrashing through the mud.

Michael Jackson

Before he could start a family, Michael had to complete a tour to promote his album, *HIStory: Past, Present and Future-Book 1.* Beginning in Prague, Czech Republic, the tour would end up selling more concert tickets than any of his tours.

Wanting to put the past behind him, the title of this album aptly pronounced to the world that Michael expected it to be the beginning of a new stage in both his personal life and musical career. During the thirteen-month tour he would perform eighty-two concerts in fifty-eight cities, ending the tour in Durban, South Africa.

When the tour ended he had something to be happy about. Debbie Rowe was six months pregnant with his child. Rowe had met Michael while working as a nurse for his dermatologist,

Dr. Arnold Klein. Katherine Jackson was not pleased to hear this when Michael told her. As a devout Jehovah's Witness, she was deeply concerned about a baby being born outside the sanctity of marriage. She reminded Michael of his half sister, Joh'Vonnie, who had been born to a woman Joseph had had an affair with years previously. She knew Michael well enough to know he would not want to do anything that reminded him of his own father.

Debbie said she had agreed to have a child for Michael because she cared deeply for him and understood his strong desire to be a father. She hadn't initially been interested in marrying Michael, but agreed to marriage after talking with Katherine. Debbie would never admit to having any romantic feelings for Michael. She described her feelings for him as being bigger and more important than romance.

Michael arranged to have Debbie meet him in Australia where he was on tour. On November 13, 1996, dressed in black, he sat before a grand piano in his suite and played "Here Comes the Bride" as Debbie, also dressed in black, stepped into the room to marry him. After exchanging vows and a brief kiss, Michael thanked her tenderly. One week later, Debbie flew back to her home in Los Angeles to prepare for the birth of Michael's son.

Michael's son was born in February 1997 in Los Angeles, California. In honor of both his grandfather and great-grandfather, Michael named his son Prince. "I have been blessed beyond comprehension and I will work tirelessly at being the best father I can be," he announced in a statement to the public shortly after the birth. Debbie handed the baby over to Michael and was rarely a presence in her son's life after that, having signed over custody rights to Michael. In April of 1998,

Michael and Debbie Rowe pose for
a wedding photo shortly after their
quiet ceremony on November 14, 1996.
(Courtesy of Reuters/HO/Landov)

she gave birth to Michael's daughter, Paris Katherine Michael Jackson, again signing away her custody rights to her daughter. In 1999 Michael and Debbie agreed to divorce.

Prince Michael and Paris were joined by Prince Michael II in 2002, whose mother's identity has never been revealed. Prince Michael II became known as "Blanket," which was a term of endearment Michael often used for "blessing." A staff of six nannies and six nurses were assigned to tend to the children in their infant years. The team worked around the clock so that at any given time each child always had two nurses and two nannies in attendance. When Michael was not available, the specially trained nannies were in charge of daily exercise and at night the nannies would read and sing to them. Air quality in the nursery was checked hourly, and utensils were boiled before being used and then thrown away after a single use.

Debbie, true to her word, stayed out of the children's lives but was granted two visits a year. It was agreed that too many visits could only confuse Prince and Paris should they get to know her as their mother. In 1999, after the divorce was final, Michael paid Debbie a $10 million settlement.

During these early years of fatherhood, Michael reconciled with Lisa. He had always cared deeply for Lisa and asked for her blessing before he married Debbie. Lisa understood Michael's intense need to become a father and also knew it was healthy not to be bitter and hold grudges. The two reconciled and Lisa joined Michael for a portion of the *HIStory* tour. She always would maintain that they had shared a genuine relationship but was never certain, however, if he had ever truly loved her. She explained, "I don't know how much he can access love, really. I think as much as he can love somebody, he might have loved me."

Ironically, Michael's new sense of confidence concerned Lisa. It was as though he felt that nothing could harm him and that he was not beholden to any obligations or responsibilities. She knew that if she became too involved with Michael a second time, her health and mental stability would suffer. "In another world, we would be together," she would say, "just not in his world, I'm afraid."

Michael had growing problems in other parts of his life. He seemed unable to control his spending and was sinking further and further into debt. Also, he was developing a reputation for not following through on his word. He would announce plans to build theme parks in various countries and then never follow through with these promises. He did not always follow through on agreements to perform concerts. Adding to his problems, the sales of his *HIStory* album were not as strong as he and his record company had hoped they would be.

Plans to release his *Invincible* album—which would end up being his last album—were set in motion in the year 2000. This album earned the distinction of being the most expensive recording ever. Michael received an advance of more than $40 million to produce it. When it was completed Sony Records claimed they spent another $25 million to promote the album. But Michael felt Sony did not promote the album with enough aggression. He even protested outside their office shortly after the album was released. He said publicly that he would like to leave Sony Records, but per the contract he had signed earlier, Michael could not leave Sony until they issued a "Greatest Hits" album and a box-set of many of his recordings. Further, because Sony often had advanced him money in the past, he owed Sony hundreds of millions of dollars.

The release of *Invincible* indicated what many critics had previously noted. Michael was at his best when he was able to write and produce his own music. His best track on this album, "Speechless," was the one song he was totally involved in from the beginning to the end of its production. Although critics were skeptical of his music, many of his fans still stood behind Michael. His earlier song "You Are Not Alone" had made chart history by reaching the number one position in the first week of its release.

Many of those close to Michael felt he had never recovered from the 1993 molestation charges. He was again using prescription drugs and his drive for music had diminished. He also stopped making sound business and public-relation decisions. In February 2003,

Opposite Page: Michael performing at a concert in Prague opening his *HIStory* world tour on September 7, 1996 (*Courtesy of Stanislav Peska/CTK/AP Photo*)

HIStory world tour in Seoul, South Korea October 11, 1996 (*Courtesy of Yun Jai-hyoung/AP Photo*)

he appeared in a documentary, *Living with Michael Jackson*, broadcast in the United Kingdom and the United States. In the film he was interviewed by British journalist Martin Bashir, best known for his controversial 1995 interview of Princess Diana in which she revealed her unhappiness in her marriage to Prince Charles. Michael had always been in awe of Princess Di and was eager to be interviewed by the same man who had interviewed her. He did not seem to consider how such an in-depth interview might damage his image. Apparently, he did not understand that many people would be unable to understand his odd and eccentric ways. He was accustomed to living a protected life and incapable of realizing that the public would be shocked by what they saw in the documentary.

In wanting to explain the immediate joy he felt when his daughter, Paris, was born, Michael admitted to Bashir of being so anxious to get her home that once his daughter's umbilical cord had been cut, he wrapped her in towels, with the placenta, and raced home with her. He admitted to his love for all children by stating, "If there were no children on this earth, I would jump off the balcony immediately." Some of what he said was clearly not true. For example, he told Bashir that the only plastic surgery he had ever had was just on his nose so he could breathe better.

The most damaging segment of the documentary was when he appeared on the show with a young boy who had been fighting cancer. As the young boy leaned against him, Michael explained:

I have slept in bed with many children . . .When you say 'bed', you're thinking sexual. They make that sexual; it's not sexual. We're going to sleep, I tuck them in and I put a little music on, and when it's story time, I read a book. We go to sleep with the fireplace on. I give them hot milk, you know, we have cookies. It's very charming, it's very sweet; it's what the whole world should do.

When the documentary aired, Michael was stunned. He hadn't realized how poorly he'd be portrayed. He also had talked about his father's abuse toward him and his brothers when they were children. Joseph was, by now, seventy-three years old. He and Katherine were still married, and despite his numerous affairs he had come to treasure his life with her. Joseph would admit that if he could have it to do all over again perhaps he wouldn't have been so hard on his children and would have been a more faithful husband.

Martin Bashir
(Courtesy of Nick Ut/AP Photo)

As hurtful and damaging as Bashir's documentary was for Joseph and Katherine, it actually helped to bring them closer together. They called Michael after the show and asked to spend time at Neverland with Michael and his children. The three of them agreed it was time to make amends.

Joseph and Katherine spent almost a week at Neverland, enjoying picnics and simple meals with Michael and his three children. They found Michael to be a devoted and loving father. Clearly, all three children loved him. The children were respectful, confident, and affectionate. Joseph and Katherine were quietly pleased to see that the children demonstrated musical talent. Michael, they noted, was raising his children with sound values. Once when Prince was combing his hair in the mirror, he remarked that he looked great. Michael shook his head and told him that he looked okay. He didn't want his children to become fixated on appearance as he had done.

Because the Bashir documentary had brought him closer to his parents, Michael at first thought it was a positive experience. Although he was too tired to perform on tours anymore and his body was starting to ache from arthritis in his knees and fingers, he felt renewed. He agreed to shoot a video for a song, "One More Chance," written and produced by R. Kelly in Las Vegas. But the project would never be completed. He would be arrested and charged with ten counts of lewd or lascivious acts with a child under the age of fourteen before the taping was over.

During the years 2002 and 2003, Michael had befriended the family of a young boy who had been diagnosed with an eight-pound cancerous tumor next to his kidney. The boy had let it be known he would like to meet Michael Jackson and Michael readily complied. When he discovered the family was struggling financially, he took over paying for the boy's medical bills and arranged for the transportation to and from his chemotherapy. Michael invited the entire family—two sons, one daughter, and their mother—into his life. Food, trips, money, gifts, and whatever else the family might enjoy or want, Michael provided. This was the same boy who had sat beside Michael in the interview during the documentary.

After the Bashir documentary aired the situation with the family began to change. Within a week of the broadcast, several child psychologists, teachers, and child advocates wrote to the child protection services in both Santa Barbara and Los Angeles to voice their concerns about the young boy who had appeared in the show with Michael. Dr. Carole Lieberman of Beverly Hills went so far as to file an official complaint and claimed the film had provided enough evidence to launch an investigation into the relationship. The Los Angeles Department of Child and Family Services (DCFS) agreed to investigate. Upon reviewing all evidence available at that time, DCFS closed the case, stating that the allegations of abuse were unfounded. During this same time period, both the Santa Barbara County Sheriff's Department and the Los Angeles Police Department had opened and closed their own investigations, also determining that there wasn't enough evidence to pursue matters.

Two months after the investigations were closed, the boy's family contacted Dr. Stanley Katz to inform him that they wanted to change the testimony they had provided in the previous investigations. Now they alleged that molestation had taken place. The Santa Barbara County Sheriff's Department agreed to reopen the investigation, which resulted in Michael's arrest. The trial began on February 28, 2005, and on June 4, 2005, Michael was found not guilty on all counts.

One of the most important documents to come of the trial was a report by Dr. Stanley Katz in which he explained that Michael "doesn't really qualify as a pedophile. He's just a regressed ten-year old."

The not-guilty verdict on charges of molestation was a victory for those who cared for and loved him. These same people feared he would never recover from this public humiliation. His former manager Frank Dileo worried: "This is devastating. For a guy like Michael, this is life-ruining, I'm afraid."

The forty-five days of trial and fifteen days of deliberations had broken him. Michael was checked into a Santa Barbara hospital for dehydration and exhaustion. After checking out of the hospital, he packed up his three children and left Neverland, knowing that he never would return. His beloved home had been ransacked by the police looking for evidence and it was no longer his sanctuary from the world.

Michael with his father Joseph, left, his brother Jackie, and his mother Katherine after his arraignment on child molestation charges at the Santa Maria, California, courthouse on April 30, 2004 *(Courtesy of Pool, Stephen Osman/AP Photo)*

Chapter Eleven
Expect This, Expect That

> *This is it. . . . This is the final curtain call.*
>
> Michael Jackson

After leaving the plush, private acres of Neverland, Michael and his children relocated to the hot and humid desert in the Persian Gulf. A member of Bahrain's wealthy royalty had offered Michael sanctuary once the trial had ended. Bahrain is a country that consists of a series of thirty islands and is considered to be one of the most remote countries in the world. Michael wanted to withdraw from the world and didn't want to see any family or friends.

The royal family in Bahrain was intent on making records with Michael. Over the course of Michael's stay in Bahrain, details of this contract were finalized, but Michael failed to uphold his part of the deals. He was later sued by the Prince of Bahrain for breach of the contract, and Michael settled the case out of court. His inability to stick to his word was a major concern among friends and business associates.

Michael Jackson's finances had reached a new low. Although he had earned more than $500 million in his career, he had incurred debts that threatened to ruin him. Prior to shutting down Neverland, it had cost an estimated $1.2 million a month to staff and maintain the estate. At one time his payroll for his staff of 120 people cost around $300,000 a month. His best asset was the music catalog he had purchased years ago for $47.5 million and was rumored to have increased in value substantially, three or four times the original amount. Over the years he had added to the catalog and owned the rights to an additional 400,000 songs. Sony had purchased 50 percent of the catalog and when Michael ran short on money, he used his half of the catalog as collateral to borrow $200 million. Should he fail to repay the loan, Sony would be able to claim his half of the catalog.

Michael had a faithful following of people willing to let his debt to them go unpaid. They felt it was still profitable to be associated with Michael and believed he would eventually pay them. In order to keep Neverland from foreclosure, Michael had allowed an investment group to purchase his mortgage, allowing him to technically retain possession of the estate.

A pharmacy company in Los Angeles sued him in an attempt to recover the more than $100,000 of prescription medications he had never paid for. There was a continual stream of lawsuits, averaging thirty to forty a year. Michael felt this was the natural fallout from being a celebrity. When it was suggested to him that he consider going back to doing concerts, he was dismayed with the idea, explaining, "When I go onstage, people expect a lot. They want the dancing, they want the spins and all. They want the whole package. But that's a lot of work. I don't know how much longer I can do it. I don't know when it'll just not be possible."

By August 2008, Michael was living in Las Vegas and preparing for his fiftieth birthday. He had no plans other than to spend the time with his three children, now aged eleven, ten, and six. By now he was almost always seen in a wheelchair, wearing his trademark surgical mask, baseball cap, and oversized sunglasses. His skin was peeling and his fingernails had turned a sickening brownish yellow. With a handful of bodyguards surrounding them, his children accompanied him everywhere, decked out in their colorful masks and clothing, each wearing large caps like their father. He was struggling with painful knees, back, and ankles. Those closest to him felt that he seemed to be struggling to maintain any sense of confidence and creative drive.

Although at first he had rejected the idea, he began to reconsider going on tour. He still had fans around the world clamoring for more music and more concerts. He also wanted his children to have the opportunity to watch him on stage before he became too old to perform. When he was approached by AEG, a tour promoter, to perform a series of fifty concerts at London's famous O2 arena from July 2009 to March 2010, he felt the time for his last performances had come. Knowing of Michael's recent reputation for not following through on contracts, and that his general health was questionable, the company hired a personal physician to be with Michael as he prepared and trained for this final series of concerts.

Michael's tenacity and determination had never deserted him. He worked hard in the daily rehearsals day after day, evening after evening. He wanted everything to be perfect.

Michael at a press conference
at the London O2 Arena in 2009
(Courtesy of Joel Ryan/AP Photo)

KING OF PO

MICHA

JACKSO

As he had done in his previous tours, Michael wanted to be involved in every segment of the production. From lighting to ticket sales, to extension cords and sound systems, Michael followed every detail of the pending concerts. After each rehearsal, Michael would return home so exhausted he often had trouble falling asleep.

The London concert opening was postponed a week because Michael felt the act was not quite ready. As was his custom, he filmed his dress rehearsals. He felt that perhaps the video of them would add to his music legacy. During the rehearsals, many remarked that Michael's performance was filled with his trademark incandescent energetic magic.

A known insomniac for years, Michael's inability to relax and sleep grew worse during the grueling rehearsal schedule. On the night of June 24, 2009, he returned to his rented estate in the Holmby Hills near Los Angeles after a rehearsal and complained to his personal physician, Dr. Conrad Murray, that he was in agony from a lack of sleep. Murray gave Michael two different sedatives, but when he still did not sleep the doctor administered him a dose of propoful around 10:40 A.M. the next day. Murray would later state that he had only given Michael a 25 mg dose, but combined with the earlier sedatives, lorazepam and midazolam, it may have proved to be deadly.

Propoful is not used as a sleeping aid. It is an anesthetic that is used to induce a coma in hospital patients, and therefore it requires constant monitoring after it has been administered. It slows down the heart rate, the respiratory rate, and other vital functions of the body. Once administered, the slowdown in breathing means not enough carbon dioxide can exit the body. Shortly after being injected with this drug, Michael suffered a massive cardiac arrest.

Whether anyone was monitoring Michael after the injection of the powerful anesthetic is not known. There is speculation that perhaps Michael had been left alone between the time of the injection and when Michael's bodyguard placed the call for an ambulance at 12:21 P.M. on June 25, 2009.

Marlon eulogizing his brother Michael during a memorial service for the late musician in Los Angeles, July 7, 2009 *(Courtesy of Mario Anzuoni/Reuters/Landov)*

Shortly after attempts to revive him at home were unsuccessful, Michael was raced to the hospital, where he was pronounced dead.

As his parents, brothers, and sisters rushed to his side, the world began to mourn the news of his death. Internet sites such as CNN, Wikipedia, and Google couldn't handle the massive amounts of inquiries by fans around the world. Twitter crashed, unable to keep up with the escalating exchanges of sorrow, speculation, and curiosity.

The police launched an investigation and others turned to Michael's complicated financial affairs. Michael's mother, Katherine Jackson, was awarded custody of Michael's three children. They did not get their chance to see their father perform one last time, but upon his death, their masks were removed to reveal to the public the delicate beauty of his three children. Their appearance at their father's funeral reminded many that whatever pain Michael had endured in his life, he had found hope and beauty in being a father to these three children.

Months before passing away, Michael had been able to enjoy one final proof of his appeal to his fans. When he had announced the final concert series, he was pleased with the public reaction to the news. It had been almost a decade since he had last performed in public, and he had been uncertain about the public reaction. "How about that!" he remarked when he learned that the almost 1 million tickets to the fifty concerts had sold out within three hours. "I always wanted to do music that inspires or influences another generation."

In his earlier years as a father, he had been asked by Barbara Walters on ABC's *20/20* television show how he would feel if his own son, Prince, ever admitted to wanting to follow his father's footsteps. Michael sighed at first, recalling the pain and loneliness in his life. Then his face brightened and he smiled as he explained what he would tell his son: "If you do go that way, expect this, expect that, expect this, expect that. I'd lay it all out. 'See you're going to get all this and all this and all this. Are you ready to do that?' He'll say, 'Yeah, I can't wait.' Well go! And do it better than I did it."

Michael Jackson's daughter Paris and two sons Prince Michael I (right) and Prince Michael II, also known as Blanket, at a memorial service for their father at the Staples Center in Los Angeles, July 7, 2009 (*Courtesy of Gabriel Buoys/PA Photos/Landov*)

Michael Jackson
Timeline

1958	Born August 29 in Gary, Indiana, the seventh of nine children.
1962	Joins brothers Jackie, Tito, Jermaine, and Marlon to become The Jackson 5.
1968	Makes first appearance at Harlem's Apollo Theater; the Jacksons win amateur night.
1968/69	Moves with family from Gary, Indiana, to Los Angeles.
1969	Performs on *The Ed Sullivan Show*; "I Want You Back" recorded on the album *Diana Ross Presents the Jackson 5* and hits No. 1 on the charts.
1972	Solo "Ben" hits No. 1 on the charts.
1977	Releases first solo album *Got to Be There*, which contains the hits "Got to Be There" and "Rockin' Robin."
1978	Stars in *The Wiz* as Scarecrow with Diana Ross as Dorothy.
1979	Releases *Off the Wall*; album propels him to superstar status.
1980	Wins his first Grammy for "Don't Stop 'til You Get Enough."
1982	Releases *Thriller*; album eventually sells more than 110 million copies, making Michael the biggest music star of the 1980s.
1983	Debuts moonwalk during a performance of "Billie Jean" at a Motown benefit concert; "Thriller" video airs on MTV; "Beat It" breaks MTV's color barrier with 10 million viewers.
1984	Suffers second-degree burns when his hair catches fire during the filming of a Pepsi commercial; *Thriller* receives a Grammy for Best Album.
1985	Co-writes "We Are the World;" song benefits famine relief.
1987	Releases *Bad*; album becomes international hit.

1988	Purchases Neverland Ranch; releases autobiography *Moonwalk*.
1991	Releases *Dangerous*.
1993	Accused in lawsuit of seducing and molesting a thirteen-year-old boy.
1994	Settles lawsuit out of court; marries Lisa Marie Presley.
1995	Releases the album *HIStory: Past, Present and Future-Book 1*.
1996	Splits with Presley after she files for divorce; marries dermatologist nurse Debbie Rowe.
1997	Son Prince Michael Jackson is born.
1998	Daughter Paris Katherine Michael Jackson is born.
1999	Splits with Rowe after she files for divorce.
2001	Releases *Invincible*, his last album.
2002	Prince Michael II (Blanket) is born.
2003	Interviewed by British journalist Martin Bashir for documentary "Living with Michael Jackson;" taken into custody by Santa Barbara County Sheriff's Department to face charges of child molestation.
2005	Found not guilty of all counts of molestation charges; leaves Neverland to live in Bahrain.
2009	Announces plans for *This Is It*, a series of concerts in London; dies June 25 of cardiac arrest in Los Angeles, California.

Sources

CHAPTER ONE: One Red Guitar
p. 9,   "When I found out . . ." Mikal Gilmore, "Triumph & Tragedy: The Life of Michael Jackson," *Rolling Stone*, Special Commemorative Issue, 2009, 11.

p. 11,   "knew that her polio . . ." Margo Jefferson, *On Michael Jackson* (New York: Pantheon Books, 2006), 38.

p. 14,   "you could take five . . ." J. Randy Taraborrelli, *Michael Jackson: The Magic, The Madness, The Whole Story 1958-2009* (New York: Grand Central Publishing, 2009), 14.

p. 16,   "I knew every step . . ." Gilmore, "Triumph & Tragedy: The Life of Michael Jackson," 14.

p. 20,   "They're talking bad about . . . " Taraborrelli, *Michael Jackson: The Magic*, 28.

CHAPTER TWO: My Poor Family
p. 21,   "I'm going to make . . ." Gilmore, "Triumph & Tragedy: The Life of Michael Jackson," 14.

p. 23,   "If you messed up . . ." Taraborrelli, *Michael Jackson: The Magic*, 34.

p. 24,   "My poor mother . . . poor family," Ibid., 33.

p. 26,   "Either you're a winner . . ." Ibid., 41.

p. 30,   "Please join me in . . ." Taraborrelli, *Michael Jackson: The Magic*, 53.

p. 30,   "I figured out at an . . ." Ibid., 54.

CHAPTER THREE: On His Own
p. 31,   "I don't know . . ." Taraborrelli, *Michael Jackson: The Magic*, 85.

p. 32,   "I remember falling asleep at . . ." Ibid., 58.

p. 32,   "Some musicians—Springsteen and . . ." Jefferson, *On Michael Jackson*, 53.

p. 32,   "It was Rose who instilled . . ." David Ritz, "The Bubblegum Soul Machine," *Rolling Stone*, Special Commemorative Issue, 2009, 31.

p. 33,   "You had to be close . . ." Taraborrelli, *Michael Jackson: The Magic*, 85.

p. 33,   "All the boys are . . ." Ibid., 64.

p. 33,   "fine young boys . . ." Ibid., 72.

p. 35,   "Michael was scared to . . ." Ibid., 77.

p. 36,   "I'll tell you the . . ." Ibid., 66.

p. 38,   "If anyone in show-business . . ." Ibid., 92.

p. 40,   "as long as we . . ." Ibid.

p. 41,   "They not only . . ." Gilmore, "Triumph & Tragedy: The Life of Michael Jackson," 16.

CHAPTER FOUR: Off the Wall in a Black Tuxedo

p. 44,   "I'm doing this . . ." Taraborrelli, *Michael Jackson: The Magic*, 183.

p. 44-46, "I saw a depth watching . . ." Anthony DeCurtis, "Michael Reinvents Pop," *Rolling Stone*, Special Commemorative Issue, 2009, 44.

p. 46,   "Do what you want . . ." Taraborrelli, *Michael Jackson: The Magic*, 182.

p. 47,   "he'd sit down and . . ." DeCurtis, "Michael Reinvents Pop," 44.

p. 49,   "The ballads were what . . ." Ibid., 45.

p. 49-50, "look at how much . . ." Taraborrelli, *Michael Jackson: The Magic*, 189.

p. 51,   "taught him a lesson . . ." DeCurtis, "Michael Reinvents Pop," 45.

p. 51,   "My family thought I . . ." Gilmore, "Triumph & Tragedy: The Life of Michael Jackson," 17.

p. 52,   "Style is a mode . . ." Jefferson, *On Michael Jackson*, 88.

p. 53,   "I guess I want . . ." Taraborrelli, *Michael Jackson: The Magic*, 232.

p. 54,   "You hear music in . . ." Ibid.

CHAPTER FIVE: Thriller

p. 55,   "I'm Michael Jackson . . ." Taraborrelli, *Michael Jackson: The Magic*, 191.

p. 55,   "I've worked with fifty-nine . . ." Steven Gaydos, "Quincy Left to Carry On," *Variety*, July 13, 2009, 18.

p. 56,   "Ever since I was . . ." Bryan Monroe, "Q&A: Michael Jackson in His Own Words," *Ebony*, December 2007, http://www.ebonyjet.com/culture/music/index.aspx? id=13602.

p. 58,   "write the type of . . ." Alan Light, "Dancing Into Immortality," *Rolling Stone,* Special Commemorative Issue, 2009, 53.

p. 62,   "Every shot is my . . ." Monroe, "Q&A: Michael Jackson in His Own Words."

p. 64,   "I guess God . . ." Ibid.

p. 64,   "I want to turn into . . ." Marc Lee, "Michael Jackson's Thriller, Interview with Director John Landis," *Telegraph*, June 26, 2009, http://www.telegraph.co.uk/culture/music/michael- jackson/5650626/Michael-Jacksons-Thriller- interview-with-John-Landis.html.

p. 65,   "Due to my strong . . ." Ibid.

p. 65,   "If only they could . . ." Monroe, "Q&A: Michael Jackson in His Own Words."

p. 65,   "It broke my heart . . ." Ibid.

CHAPTER SIX: One White Glove

p. 69,   "It's a difficult life . . ." Gilmore, "Triumph & Tragedy: The Life of Michael Jackson," 20.

p. 77,   "It's beyond us . . ." Bryan Monroe, "Q&A: Michael Jackson in His Own Words."

p. 79,   "You don't get peace . . ." Gerri Hirshey, "Michael Jackson: Life in the Magical Kingdom," *Rolling Stone,* February 17, 1983, http://www.rollingstone.com/news/story/22775354/ michael_jackson_life_in_the_magical_kingdom/print.

p. 80,   "In some ways . . ." Hirshey, "Michael Jackson: Life in the Magical Kingdom."

p. 80,   "a self-created piece . . ." Matthews Cox & Associates, "Yale Conference Examines Life, Work of Michael Jackson," *Black Issues in Higher Education,* October 21, 2004, 13.

CHAPTER SEVEN: Who Is the Man in the Mirror?

p. 81,   "They called Elvis . . ." Taraborrelli, *Michael Jackson: The Magic,* 374.

p. 81-82, "I wake up from . . ." Hirshey, "Michael Jackson: Life in the Magical Kingdom."

p. 82,   "The closer he gets . . ." Taraborrelli, *Michael Jackson: The Magic,* 367.

p. 82,   "You can't think about . . ." Michael Goldberg and David Handelman, "Is Michael Jackson for Real?," *Rolling Stone,* September 24, 1987.

p. 82,   "the oldest man I . . ." Ibid.

p. 85,   "We can actually control . . ." Taraborrelli, *Michael Jackson: The Magic,* 360.

p. 85,   "Michael is one of . . ." Ibid.

p. 87,   "Out of everyone . . ." Ibid., 433.

p. 90,   "These people are going . . ." Taraborrelli, *Michael Jackson: The Magic,* 421.

CHAPTER EIGHT: Neverland

p. 91,   "My guests expect . . ." Taraborrelli, *Michael Jackson: The Magic,* 384.

p. 91,   "With Michael, as with . . ." Michael Goldberg, "Michael Jackson's 'Dangerous Mind,' *Rolling Stone,* January 9, 1992, http://www.rollingstone.com/news/story/5939818/cover story_michael_jackson_dangerous_mind/print.

p. 94,   "Might be armed . . ." Paul Theroux, "My Trip to Neverland, and the Call from Michael Jackson I'll Never Forget," *Telegraph,* June 27, 2009.

p. 95,   "Neverland isn't about kids . . ." Michael Goldberg, "Michael Jackson's 'Dangerous Mind.'"

p. 98,   "There's a vulnerability . . ." Theroux, "My Trip to Neverland, and the Call from Michael Jackson I'll Never Forget."

p. 99,   "the juxtaposition of sex . . ." Goldberg, "Michael Jackson's 'Dangerous Mind.'"

p. 99,   "All I had to yell . . ." Ibid.

p. 100,   "Of course he loved . . ." Touré, "Black Superhero," *Rolling Stone,* Special Commemorative Issue, 2009, 73.

CHAPTER NINE: Marriage, Children, and $20 Million

p. 103,   "Michael has a lot . . ." Hirshey, "Michael Jackson: Life in the Magical Kingdom."

p. 103,   "Children know a lot . . ." Taraborrelli, *Michael Jackson: The Magic*, 450.

p. 104,   "the least weird man . . ." Ibid., 454.

p. 108,   "I started falling for . . ." Ibid., 510.

p. 108,   "I need to start . . . life back," Ibid., 528.

p. 109,   "I ask all of you . . ." Ibid., 539.

p. 109,   "I actually did fall . . ." Ibid., 553.

p. 110,   "if they want . . ." Ibid., 563.

CHAPTER TEN: HIStory

p. 113,   "Why does everyone . . ." Taraborrelli, *Michael Jackson: The Magic*, 632.

p. 114,   "I have been blessed . . ." Ibid., 590.

p. 116,   "I don't know how . . ." Brian Hiatt, "What Went Wrong," *Rolling Stone*, Special Commemorative Issue, 2009, 85.

p. 117,   "In another world, we . . ." Taraborrelli, *Michael Jackson: The Magic*, 599.

p. 120,   "If there were no . . ." Ibid., 603.

p. 120-21, "I have slept in . . ." Ibid., 606.

p. 124,   "doesn't really qualify as . . ." Ibid., 648.

p. 124,   "This is devastating . . ." Ibid., 69.

CHAPTER ELEVEN: Expect This, Expect That

p. 125,   "This is it . . ." "Michael Jackson Announces 10-Concert Run at London's O2 Arena," Rock&Roll Daily, Rolling Stone online, March 5, 2009, http://www.rollingstone.com/rockdaily/index.php/2009/03/05/michael-jackson-announces-ten-concert-run-at-londons-o2-arena/.

p. 126-27, "When I go onstage, people . . ." Taraborrelli, *Michael Jackson: The Magic*, 693.

p. 132,   "I always wanted . . ." Ryan Monroe, "Q&A: Michael Jackson in His Own Words."

p. 132,   "If you do go . . ." "Michael Jackson Reveals That He Feels Imprisoned By the Paparazzi," *Jet*, October 6, 1997, 35.

Bibliography

Belluck, Pam. "Jackson's Health a Subject of Confusion."
    New York Times, June 27, 2009.
Brown, Mick. "Michael Jackson, Death by Showbusiness."
    Telegraph, June 27, 2009. http:// www.telegraph.co.uk/culture/music/
    michael-j ackson/5659778/Michael-Jackson-death-by- showbusiness.html.
Collins, Gail. "Michael, A Foreign Affair."
    New York Times, July 6, 2009.
Cox, Matthews & Associates. "Yale Conference Examines Life, Work of
    Michael Jackson." *Black Issues In Higher Education,* October 21, 2004.
Dahl, Bill. *Motown: The Golden Years.* Iola, Wis.: Krause
    Publications, 2001.
DeCurtis, Anthony. "Michael Reinvents Pop." *Rolling
    Stone,* Special Commemorative Issue, 2009.
Dolan, Jon. "King of Pain." *Rolling Stone,* Special
    Commemorative Issue, 2009.
Fong-Torres, Ben. "Cover Story: The Jackson 5: The Men Don't Know But the
    Little Girls Understand." *Rolling Stone,* April 29, 1971.
Gates, David, and Raina Kelley. "Finding Neverland,
    Michael Jackson's Life." *Newsweek,* July 13, 2009.
Gaydos, Steven. "Quincy Left To Carry On." *Variety,* July 13, 2009.
———. *The Rolling Stone Encyclopedia of Rock & Roll,*
    Third Edition. Edited by Holly George-Warren and
    Patricia Romanowski. New York: Fireside, 2001.
Gilmore, Mikal. "Triumph & Tragedy: The Life of Michael
    Jackson." *Rolling Stone,* Special Commemorative Issue, 2009.
Goldberg, Michael. "Michael Jackson's 'Dangerous Mind.'"
    Rolling Stone, January 9, 1992.
    http://www.rollingstone.com/news/story/5939818/cover_story_
    michael_jackson_dngerous_mind/print.
Goldberg, Michael, and Christopher Connelly. "Trouble In Paradise?"
    Rolling Stone, March 15, 1984. http://www.rollingstone.com/news/
    story/28852599/trouble_in_paradise/print.
Goldberg, Michael, and David Handelman. "Cover Story:
    Is Michael Jackson for Real?" *Rolling Stone,* September 24, 1987.
Haskins, James. *Black Music in America: A History
    Through Its People.* New York: T. Y. Crowell, 1987.
Hiatt, Brian. "What Went Wrong." *Rolling Stone,* Special
    Commemorative Issue, 2009.
Hirshey, Gerri. "Michael Jackson: Life in the Magical Kingdom."*Rolling
    Stone,* February 17, 1983. http://www.rollingstone.com/news/
    story/22775354/michael _jackson_life_in_the_magical_kingdom/print.
Hoskyns, Barney. "Blame It On The Good Times: Michael Jackson's Genius
    Lay In Transmuting Black Music Into A Global Form. His Tragedy
    Was That He Forgot What Made Him Great." *New Statesman,* 1996.
Jefferson, Margo. *On Michael Jackson.* New York:
    Pantheon Books, 2006.
———. "Michael Jackson Reveals That He Feels
    Imprisoned By The Paparazzi." *Jet,* October 6, 1997.
———. "Jackson Refutes Molestation Charges; Maintains Views On Sleeping
    With Kids During '60 Minutes Interview.'" *Jet,* January 19, 2004.
Jones, Quincy. "Remembering Michael." *Newsweek,* July 13, 2009.

Lee, Marc. "Michael Jackson's Thriller, Interview With
Director John Landis." *Telegraph,* June 26, 2009. http://www.
telegraph.co.uk/culture/music/michael-jackson/5650626/AMichael-
Jacksons-Thriller-interview-with-John-Landis.html.

Light, Alan. "Dancing Into Immortality." *Rolling Stone,*
Special Commemorative Issue, 2009.

Macaulay, Alastair. "His Moves Expressed As Much As His
Music." *New York Times,* June 27, 2009.

Mabry, Marcus. "In Jackson's Death, Black Ambivalence
Fades." *New York Times,* June 29, 2009.

Monroe, Bryan. "Q&A: Michael Jackson In His Own
Words." *Ebony,* December 2007.

———. "Time Gap Could Prove To Be Key To Jackson Case." MSNBC.
com, August 26, 2009. http://www.msnbc.msn.com/id/32564402/ns/
entertainment-music/print/1/displaymode/1098.

Pareles, Jon. "Tricky Steps From Boy To Superstar." *New
York Times,* June 26, 2009.

Phinney, Kevin. *Souled America: How Black Music
Transformed White Culture.* New York: Billboard Books, 2005.

Rawlinson, Linnie, and Nick Hunt. "Jackson Dies, Almost
Takes Internet With Him." CNN.com, June 26, 2009. http://cnn.site.
printthis.clickability.com/pt/cpt?action=cpt&title=Jackson+dies
%2C+almost+takes+Internet+with+him/html.

Ritz, David. "The Bubblegum Soul Machine." *Rolling
Stone,* Special Commemorative Issue, 2009.

Ruth, Daniel. "Jackson's Weirdness Part of the Story, Too." *St. Petersburg
Times,* July 10, 2009.

Sandomir, Richard. "How Jackson Redefined The Super
Bowl." *New York Times,* June 30, 2009.

Segal, David. "Fame May Never Be The Same." *New York
Times,* June 28, 2009.

Shaw, Arnold. *Black Popular Music in America.* New York:
Schirmer Books, 1986.

Sheffield, Rob. "A New Kind of Musical." *Rolling Stone,*
Special Commemorative Issue, 2009.

———. "When Michael Became Michael." *Rolling Stone,*
Special Commemorative Issue, 2009.

Sisario, Ben. "Sales of Michael Jackson's Music,
Downloads and CDs, Stay Strong." *New York Times,* July 16, 2009.

Sorkin, Andrew Ross, and Michael J. De la Merced.
"Jackson Assets Draw the Gaze of Wall Street." *New York Times,* July
20, 2009.

Taraborrelli, J. Randy. *Michael Jackson: The Magic, The
Madness, the Whole Story 1958-2009.* New York: Grand Central
Publishing, 2009.

Theroux, Paul. "My Trip to Neverland, And the Call From
Michael Jackson I'll Never Forget." *Telegraph,* June 27, 2009.
http://www.telegraph.co.uk/culture/music/michael-jackson/ My-Trip-
to-Neverland.html.

Touré. "Black Superhero." *Rolling Stone,* Special Commemorative Issue, 2009.

———. "Jackson Life Evokes Praise, Controversy." *USA Today,* July 10, 2009.

Web sites

http://www.rollingstone.com/news/story/28852664/rolling_stones_essential_michael_jackson_coverage
Find almost everything there is to know about Michael Jackson here on the Web site of *Rolling Stone* magazine. You'll find a biography, archived articles, videos, album reviews, a photo gallery, and lots more.

http://www.topics.nytimes.com/top/reference/timestopics/people/j/michael_jackson/
The *New York Times* covered Michael extensively, from his early days as a Motown child star to his untimely death, and this site provides full coverage of his life and times.

http://www.latimes.com
Type in the name Michael Jackson on the *Los Angeles Times* site and more than six hundred results will show up, including everything from an interactive timeline to videos.

Book cover and interior design by Derrick Carroll.

Index